T0052639

Tocqueville: A Very Short Introduction

Very Short Introductions available now:

THE UNITED NATIONS
    Jussi M. Hanhimäki
THE VIKINGS Julian Richards
WITCHCRAFT Malcolm Gaskill
WITTGENSTEIN A. C. Grayling

WORLD MUSIC Philip Bohlman
THE WORLD TRADE
    ORGANIZATION Amrita Narlikar
WRITING AND SCRIPT
    Andrew Robinson

Available soon:

LANDSCAPES AND
    GEOMORPHOLOGY
    Andrew Goudie and Heather Viles
SPANISH LITERATURE Jo Labanyi
DIPLOMACY Joesph M. Siracusa

NORTH AMERICAN INDIANS
    Theda Perdue and
    Michael D. Green
THE U.S. CONGRESS
    Donald A. Ritchie

For more information visit our web site
www.oup.co.uk/general/vsi/

Harvey C. Mansfield

TOCQUEVILLE

A Very Short Introduction

OXFORD
UNIVERSITY PRESS

Oxford University Press, Inc., publishes works that further
Oxford University's objective of excellence
in research, scholarship, and education.

Oxford   New York
Auckland   Cape Town   Dar es Salaam   Hong Kong   Karachi
Kuala Lumpur   Madrid   Melbourne   Mexico City   Nairobi
New Delhi   Shanghai   Taipei   Toronto

With offices in
Argentina   Austria   Brazil   Chile   Czech Republic   France   Greece
Guatemala   Hungary   Italy   Japan   Poland   Portugal   Singapore
South Korea   Switzerland   Thailand   Turkey   Ukraine   Vietnam

Copyright © 2010 by Harvey C. Mansfield

Published by Oxford University Press, Inc.
198 Madison Avenue, New York, NY 10016

www.oup.com

Oxford is a registered trademark of Oxford University Press

Library of Congress Cataloging-in-Publication Data
Mansfield, Harvey Claflin, 1932–
Tocqueville : a very short introduction / Harvey C. Mansfield.
p.   cm.
ISBN 978-0-19-517539-4 (pbk.)
1. Tocqueville, Alexis de, 1805–1859—Political and social views.
2. Historians—France—Biography.
3. Statesmen—France—Biography.
4. Democracy.   I. Title.
JC229.T8.M33 2010
320.092—dc22   [B]
2010010473

Printed by Integrated Books International, United States of America
on acid-free paper

Acknowledgments

This volume is sponsored by the Taskforce on the Virtues of a Free Society of the Hoover Institution at Stanford University, where I am the Carol G. Simon Senior Fellow. Support for it came also from a research fellowship at the Carl Friedrich von Siemens Foundation in Munich, Germany, held for the first six months of 2009 at the invitation of my longtime friend Dr. Heinrich Meier. Nor must I forget the everyday generosity of Harvard University, where I have essentially spent my life. I am grateful to Kathryn Sensen for invaluable and unsparing criticism of the text served with all due respect. My late wife, Delba Winthrop, who would have been co-author of the book, was ever in my thoughts as I composed it.

Contents

List of illustrations

Introduction: a new kind of liberal

What sort of man was Alexis de Tocqueville? A writer, certainly, and with great style, but a writer of nonfiction conveying fact and truth in compelling terms with brilliant formulations. A social scientist, but without the cumbersome methodology, the hands-off neutrality, the pretended objectivity of today's version. Tocqueville was a defender and reformer of politics, scientific in some ways but never permitting science to obstruct those goals. A historian? Yes, because he wrote of democracy in America, then and now its principal abode, and of the old regime in France, where according to him democracy—surprisingly, in the form of rational administration by a monarchy—began. He did not write like a theorist, as if he were abstracted from time and place. Yet he was a seeker of causes, not a plain narrator, and he chose to write about the most important events, the "first causes," he went so far as to say. A philosopher? A difficult question, to which many who identify philosophy with system say no. I say yes, more of a philosopher than he appears to be. We can settle on "thinker," a less ambitious word for a man who had his doubts about philosophy.

A great man? For certain. A great man for his insight, but also because he undertook to explain greatness in a democratic age when it was under attack or simply overlooked. A great man who associated democracy and liberty with greatness.

1. Alexis de Tocqueville in 1850. When Tocqueville was born, his father took one look at his extraordinarily expressive face and said that he was sure to be a great man.

"A new kind of liberal": that is Tocqueville's own description of himself. Today Tocqueville is not known as a liberal, as is his friend John Stuart Mill, who wrote *On Liberty* to explain and advocate liberal principles. Tocqueville seems to be more descriptive and analytical, like a sociologist, except that he writes so well. Although his books sparkle with insights, his thoughts arise from observation of facts rather than appearing in the sequence of argument, arranged systematically. But I shall try to rescue his own label for himself and show that he deserves the highest rank among liberals *just because* he is not as theoretical as liberals normally want to be.

If Tocqueville is a new kind of liberal, this means that liberalism is not itself something new. It is true that the word "liberal" came into use only in Tocqueville's time, but before this liberalism was given its basis in the doctrine of modern political theorists in the seventeenth century, particularly Thomas Hobbes, Baruch Spinoza, and John Locke, who made it their first premise that man was naturally free. They meant that prior to any social or political character men might have, man must be supposed to be in an abstract condition (the "state of nature") in which he was free to consent to the society he might join and to its politics. Tocqueville did not agree that men began in this way "perfectly free," as Locke said, or that freedom has its origin prior to politics. Tocqueville seems rather to agree with Aristotle, the pre-modern philosopher opposed by these modern theorists, who said that "man is by nature a political animal," meaning that human freedom has to be found in politics, not in an original state of nature prior to politics.

Tocqueville does not say he agrees with Aristotle. He does not agree with him that philosophy is the highest way of life. He does not argue with philosophers and rarely refers to them; when he does, it is usually to disparage them. In *Democracy in America,* the Americans he praises for the practice of freedom are said to be "less occupied with philosophy" than any other civilized people. In

The Old Regime and the Revolution he decries the *philosophes* or "men of letters" of the Enlightenment in the eighteenth century for pronouncing on politics as theorists, without experience in the practice of politics. In neither work does he mention the liberal state of nature, and in his book on America he omits any discussion of the liberal American principles stated in the Declaration of Independence. Tocqueville is obviously aware of the old liberalism, but he deals with it by ignoring it.

Instead, he moves to his new liberalism in which freedom is the friend of religion and infused with pride as well as impelled by self-interest. The new liberalism needs a "new political science...for a world that is altogether new," not set forth in a system of principles by Tocqueville, comparable to the system of seventeenth-century liberalism. Nor is it the political science of Montesquieu, the more modern political scientist of the eighteenth century, authoritative for fellow liberals in Tocqueville's time such as Benjamin Constant and François Guizot, and earlier for the American authors of *The Federalist*. Montesquieu's new political science was written for the world before the coming of modern democracy that made a world "altogether new," before the United States came to be.

Tocqueville's political science is shown in his depiction of freedom as practiced in America, an actual society, rather than in principles that precede practice. That is why his writing fascinates and convinces his readers with evidence, observation, and examples. Yet his analysis, often apparently spontaneous, even disorderly, does not wander from one point to another; every discussion has its place in a whole that is gradually revealed. In this book I discuss five aspects of his new liberalism. All are somehow concerned with democracy, for democracy is the new world in which liberty must be made to survive and prosper.

First is the democratic politics in Tocqueville's own life, for he was a would-be statesman as well as a writer, and a liberal as well as an aristocrat. Then come his thoughts on democratic self-government in America, where in his time and still in ours democracy has its headquarters. His fears for democracy come next, found especially in the second volume of *Democracy in America*. There he exposes the risks arising from democratic theories that both exasperate and enervate democratic majorities. Then, moving to *The Old Regime*, we find Tocqueville's depiction of the rational administrative control by which the French monarchy dismantled feudal aristocracy. He reveals the connection between two things that seem some distance apart: democracy (rule of the people) and rational administration (rule of a bureaucracy). Last is the greatness Tocqueville desires from democracy, such as it can be. For democracy is given to mediocrity that is both stagnant and restive, passive yet dissatisfied, and Tocqueville must teach us how to rescue it from its faults. For him the "true friends" of liberty are also friends of "human greatness."

Why does Tocqueville matter today? First, there is general agreement that he matters. It is hard to think of any analyst of American politics and society with a higher or broader reputation today. During his own life and then through the nineteenth century and most of the twentieth, his liberalism seemed humdrum and ineffective, and he was eclipsed by radical critics on both left and right. But after the radical right was defeated in World War II and the radical left lost its appeal in the nastiness of communist tyranny, moderate liberals came to the fore, above all Tocqueville. In France the revival was led by the philosopher Raymond Aron and the historian François Furet; in the United States, having always been celebrated for his book, Tocqueville returned to favor as Americans reconsidered their intellectual dependence on Marx and Nietzsche and began again to discuss the nature of "American exceptionalism," by which America might be a model for all humanity. He has been quoted by every American president from Eisenhower on (not always accurately!), cited widely in academic circles by social scientists and historians, and used to enliven and give authority to many books by popular historians and journalists. *Democracy in America* also appeals broadly to both left and right, each side having its favorite passages and eager to claim the blessing of his authority.

Tocqueville has not received his due for the quality of his thought, however. One reason is his very brilliance, which makes him seem merely eloquent, and his sense of the future, which makes him seem uncanny. It is as if anyone who writes so well on the surface must be superficial, and anyone who predicts so well must be a seer. The beauty of his writing can be somewhat distracting to careful analysis of what he says, as for example when he compares a presidential election in America to the passing of a storm. Another reason for the underestimation of his wisdom is the power of abstraction in democratic societies, a power Tocqueville tries to oppose. American democrats like to generalize, or universalize, or equalize, so as to be inclusive, tolerant, and appreciative. America's intellectuals, cooperating with the democrats, like to theorize, so as to be universal, exact, and free of the past. Even our historians want to start history anew. Tocqueville's liberalism forces us to consider what we actually do in the practice of self-government, rather than arguing endlessly in the abstract about what we are, and are not, entitled to. For all his reputation, we do not learn enough from him.

Chapter 1
Tocqueville's democratic providence

Born not long after the French Revolution into an old aristocratic family of Normandy, Alexis de Tocqueville lived from July 29, 1805, until April 16, 1859. He was bound to the ancien régime, the Old Regime, by his family and to the new one by his belief in liberty. He lived through the coming of democracy to France and foresaw that it would eventually spread to all the world. His

2. Château de Tocqueville in Normandy. Tocqueville lived at the family chateau but did not leave an heir to inherit it.

family name was Clérel, and one of the Clérels had fought with William the Conqueror at the battle of Hastings in 1066. By stages the family acquired the fief of Tocqueville in Normandy and in 1661 took that name. The chateau still exists and is inhabited by descendants of his brother.

3. Mary ("Marie") Mottley, Tocqueville's wife, ca. 1830. English, Protestant, and middle-class, she was an unusual choice of wife for a French aristocrat, but Tocqueville wrote to her that "you are without exception the only person in the world who knows the bottom of my soul."

Alexis kept his title and lived in his beloved chateau, but although he spent much time and money caring for it, he did not produce an heir to inherit it. It was an accident he did not regret, and he once said that he had "no very keen desire to draw from the great lottery of paternity." This view of paternity reveals a mixture of aristocratic disdain for the common man, democratic unconcern for the future of one's family, and philosophic equanimity. His marriage, however, was more simply democratic. He married beneath himself, as he acknowledged, to an Englishwoman not of the nobility (and on whom he insisted, despite the wishes of some in his family).

Tocqueville the statesman

Tocqueville refused to use the title of Count, but he did not reject all the advantages of aristocratic birth. He made them serve a democratic end in what he called the "new world" of democracy. Although he lived his life as an aristocrat, he took the part of democracy and to do so, he entered the practice of politics. In aristocracy as it should have been in the Old Regime in France, he would have claimed power by feudal inheritance. Entering politics, Tocqueville believed, was in its nature aristocratic for the simple reason that governing requires taking responsibility for others, thus being superior to them. His first experience in politics under the Restoration monarchy came from a touch of privilege, for Tocqueville's father, Hervé, had been a prefect and active in local government. Through his advice and influence, Alexis became an unpaid apprentice judge in 1827. After that he had to run for office in—somewhat—democratic elections. Here we see two of his principles at work: the democratization of politics that is essentially and originally aristocratic; and learning politics by doing politics, which was the particular virtue he found in American democracy. The two principles converge, because politics can be democratized only if democrats make a virtue of competing for the offices that would have belonged to the nobles of an aristocracy without effort. One of Tocqueville's greatest insights was to see that this virtue, necessary to democracy, cannot be taken for granted in a democracy and may actually be threatened there.

Entering politics in Tocqueville's time was a daunting task. After the French Revolution, government in France was transformed by a series of spastic lurches from the Bourbon monarchy before 1789, the "Old Regime," to the constitutional republic; then to the Jacobin republic of terror; to the Thermidor reaction against the Jacobins; to Napoleon's empire; to the Bourbon monarchy restored; to the bourgeois monarchy of Louis-Philippe; to the Second Republic, which was subverted and overthrown by Louis Napoleon, who established a second empire. Such turbulence promised risk for any ambitious person who might have wanted to enter politics and anguish for any concerned observer. For a writer and thinker like Tocqueville, it would have readily excused the renunciation of politics for the sake of relief and refuge in private life, providing leisure for thinking and for indulging his superb talent for writing. But Tocqueville, who felt anguish for France all his life, took up every opportunity for political activity even when doing so interfered with his writing, as in 1837 when he could have been working on the second volume of *Democracy in America* and instead ran for office in the Chamber of Deputies in the regime of Louis-Philippe. Though he was defeated the first time, despite being a noble running in his own locality, he tried again in 1839—manfully and with democratic resolve—and succeeded, then was reelected twice more. After the fall of Louis-Philippe's monarchy in 1848, Tocqueville was elected to the Constituent Assembly that was intended to establish the Second Republic, helping to prepare its constitution. Then he was elected to the new assembly under that constitution and served as Minister of Foreign Affairs for five months, until the cabinet of which he was a member was dismissed by the new president, Louis Napoleon. In December 1851, Louis Napoleon put an end to the republic with a coup d'état, and Tocqueville left politics for good, having stayed with it as long as his principles required and permitted. His last political experience was being jailed for two days as a protesting deputy by Louis Napoleon.

What was it that made this born writer enter democratic politics where he himself doubted he could succeed? For Tocqueville the freedom to write and publish was incomplete without political freedom. He wanted to feel that freedom for himself by holding office rather than merely observe from outside. It was not enough to understand things with calm detachment, as a theorist would. He believed that the satisfaction and serenity of soul, said in the philosophic tradition to reward the activity of contemplation, do not exist. He thought the human soul, and especially his own, to be "restive and insatiable." He despised "all the goods of this world," yet to escape the "grievous numbness" that comes over the soul when it tries to contemplate itself, he sought those goods. The principal good was of course honor, the "natural taste" he had for "great actions and great virtues"; all the others were subordinate, merely means to honor. Consciously, deliberately, purposefully, Tocqueville wished and acted to distinguish himself in life, at the same time disdaining honor and reaching for it.

Tocqueville seemed to understand the love of distinction as essentially political—the activity of ruling—rather than literary in the sense of displaying talent and intelligence for the sake of popular esteem. Yet he thought he was "more worthy in thought than in action," and he was surely right about that. As a politician he lacked the common touch, and he knew it. He confessed (privately, in his *Recollections* [*Souvenirs*]) that he could hardly remember the names and faces of the mediocre men in the National Assembly with whom he had to deal: "they bore me profoundly." He also said that writing was a kind of action, a way of engaging in politics. It seems that political freedom for Tocqueville has two branches—holding office and writing—and that they converge in greatness.

For a philosopher, or for most philosophers, human greatness is a small thing, a self-inflation of man bound to lose size and value in proportion to eternity. Not so for Tocqueville. "My imagination," he said in a letter, "easily climbs to the summit of human greatness." It was not that he thought himself another Alexander, but he felt dissatisfied with worldly honors, the same ones he pursued, yet uncertain that God assured the greatness of man. The restiveness in his soul had aristocratic pride in its disdain and at the same time democratic responsibility for undertaking political tasks that aristocratic hierarchy would now, under democracy, no longer be able to accomplish.

Tocqueville the writer

Honorable failure was the best Tocqueville could do as statesman, and the rest of his life must be seen as events in the career of a writer. Indeed, his most exciting political experience was to observe and record the two revolutions in France that occurred in the wake of the French Revolution, in 1830 and 1848. As a judge in 1830 he had to decide whether to swear an oath of allegiance to the new Orleanist king, renouncing the legitimate Bourbon heir—which he did. In January 1848 he gave a speech warning the government of the coming revolution, but though a member of the Chamber of Deputies, he could accomplish no more than this warning, and he was forced to watch impotently as the Second Republic was being born, which he did with grave misgivings for its socialist future. In 1850, while suffering from the tuberculosis that was to kill him, he wrote his *Recollections* on that revolution, a kind of "day-dreaming," he said, intended for his friends and perhaps for eventual publication (not until 1893, as it turned out). Here was his moment near the cockpit of the democratic revolution whose study occupied his life, but all he could do was watch and write. But that he did to great effect.

Tocqueville's early education was provided by the Abbé Lesueur, who had been his father's tutor. Lesueur gave him an old-fashioned religious training but otherwise pampered him, and the two became close friends. When he was sixteen, his father, then prefect in Metz, sent him to a college to study rhetoric and philosophy. At this time, Tocqueville recounted later, he went to his father's library and there found books of philosophy that produced an "earthquake" inside him, allowing a "universal doubt" to penetrate his soul, previously full of faith. The doubt, with which he struggled for the rest of his life, undermined his faith not

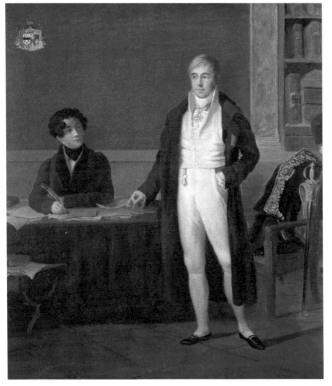

4. Tocqueville, age sixteen or seventeen, sits at a desk beside his father, Hervé de Tocqueville, 1822.

only in God but also in the "intellectual world" of "all the truths" he had constructed for his beliefs and actions.

Ignoring the earthquake in the soul of his son, Tocqueville's father sent him to study law in Paris, which he did from 1823 to 1826. Two years later he attended lectures by François Guizot, later premier of France, and took notes showing that he was impressed by Guizot's thoughts on the history of mankind or "civilization." In a letter of the time he calls his works "prodigious" in ideas and words. Guizot and Benjamin Constant were the two great French liberals of the early nineteenth century with whom Tocqueville is often compared. But the two of them believed, quite unlike Tocqueville, that liberalism could hold democracy in check without having to come to terms with it. Whatever Tocqueville learned from them did not reach this main point. Yet here was an episode of classroom contact he had with the most advanced liberal thinking of his day.

For the most part, however, Tocqueville's education was his own reading of the historians of his time and in the classics of political philosophy. His favorites were French, "three men with whom I live a little every day," he said in 1836—Pascal, Montesquieu, and Rousseau. But in addition to authors whom he read he had friends to whom he wrote extensively, and he taught himself by teaching his friends. Among these were the literary scholar J.-J. Ampère, the social theorist Arthur de Gobineau, the English economist Nassau Senior, the statesman Pierre-Paul Royer-Collard, his particular intimates Francisque de Corcelle, Madame Sophie Swetchine, Adolphe de Circourt, Eugène Stöffels, and his friend from childhood, Louis de Kergorlay.

Above all was the friendship of Tocqueville with Gustave de Beaumont, to whom he wrote three volumes of letters and with whom he made his nine-month trip to America (1831–32) preceding the writing of *Democracy in America*. They had studied law together and served as magistrates on the same court, and attended Guizot's lectures before their celebrated trip. They went to America to see "what a great republic is," said Tocqueville in a letter, apparently with a vague idea of a joint project. Their more definite plan was to write a book on penal reform in America. Though that was but a "pretext" (as Tocqueville confided to Kergorlay), the two delivered a book on the subject (*On the Penitentiary System in the United States and Its Application to France*) a year after their return from America, in which they approved of reform but, in a way characteristic of Tocqueville's liberalism, reproved the exaggerated hopes of reformers.

Tocqueville and Beaumont circled through most of America as it then was. They began from New York and went north through Buffalo to the Great Lakes and to Michigan and Wisconsin, where the frontier was. The "frontier" was the boundary between nature and civilization, and while he was there, writing "on the steamboat," Tocqueville produced a brief but beautiful reflection on the silence of nature and the varied talk of civilization, comparing Americans with English and French, and considering the Indians as humans outside and hostile to civilization. *Fortnight in the Wilderness* (1831, when Tocqueville was twenty-six) was written for publication but not published until after his death.

Both Tocqueville and Beaumont kept journals during their trip, and though Tocqueville's was published as *Journey to America*, it consisted of unconnected notes for his later books and was not composed, as was *Fortnight*. At some point in the trip, the joint project for a book on the great republic in America became one for Tocqueville alone, as one may surmise was his intention all along. After testing the frontier, which they saw was only temporary and would not rest until it reached the Pacific Ocean, they went to Canada, then down to Boston, Philadelphia, and Baltimore, then west to Pittsburgh, and south to Nashville, Memphis, and New Orleans, from which they went through Georgia and the Carolinas to Washington, and at last to New York, from which they departed to France. They rode in steamboats and stayed in a log cabin. They met President Andrew Jackson briefly and talked at length with many Americans, prominent and not so prominent. Tocqueville's method of survey research was to ask questions suited to the person interviewed, listen, and probe, looking for facts and opinions, rather than to count reactions to the same set of queries as a modern social scientist would.

Democracy in America was published in two volumes five years apart, in 1835 and 1840. The first volume, more about America and its virtues and faults, was a sensational success, but the second, with its measured analysis and foreboding of the future of democracy, was received without enthusiasm. Praised by great writers of France such as Chateaubriand and Sainte-Beuve, the first volume brought fame and honor to Tocqueville. In 1838 he was made a member of the Académie des sciences morales et politiques, and in 1841, at the age of thirty-six, he was elected to the Académie française, where he kept his social life, particularly in the years under Louis Napoleon after his political life had come to an end. He gave a lecture on political science at the Académie des sciences morales et politiques in 1852, distinguishing that discipline from the "art of governing" because it centers on the logic of ideas rather than the gross commonplaces necessary for governing. But Tocqueville's political science took its logic from the commonplaces by refining them instead of opposing and refuting them as did the theorists of liberalism.

America was not the only destination for Tocqueville. He had traveled to Sicily in 1827, resulting in his first writing. After his American trip he went to England in 1833 and to England and Ireland in 1835, eager to observe the progress of democracy in the most liberal country of Europe, interested in the decentralized administration of government that he had found in America, and seeking to study the difference between the English aristocracy and the French. He also went to Switzerland (1836) and to Algeria (1841, 1846). He wrote reports on poverty (*Memoir on*

Pauperism, 1835), slavery, and the colonies. In 1850, having left politics, he undertook to write the book on the French Revolution that he had long contemplated. It was a project he did not live to complete, yet he did publish the first part, *The Old Regime and the Revolution*, in 1856. This was to be a "great work," he said in a letter to Kergorlay, a "mixture of history properly speaking with philosophical history," which would provide a broad judgment on "our modern societies" and their probable future. And he declared that he has "no cause but that of liberty and human dignity." In leaving politics he remained in politics, and in studying history he taught philosophy.

Chapter 2
Tocqueville's praise of democracy

Tocqueville does not begin by praising democracy, and he never praises it to the skies. He awards praise only as he describes it in action. He begins *Democracy in America* by saying that democracy is a fact, a "providential fact," thus stepping back from the attitudes of its promoters and its opponents (for in his day there still were opponents). Democracy is on the rise everywhere and has come to fruition in America, he states. It does not need to be promoted and it cannot be opposed. Tocqueville believes that both the promoters and the opponents do more harm than good, and especially the promoters because they are more in harmony with democratic times, hence more seductive than the reactionaries. Democracy must first be analyzed and assessed for its strengths and weaknesses, and then it can be usefully praised with a view to confirming the former and counteracting the latter. Tocqueville appraises democracy rather than assuming it to be good or the only legitimate government.

The image of democracy

What is democracy? Tocqueville defines it first as equality of conditions, as a way of life; only when he comes to the Puritans does he begin to describe it as a form of government. Democracy as a way of life is not so worthy of praise as when it means self-government. To its definition as equality of conditions we might

object that there are manifest inequalities in democracy today—
let alone in his time—to which he would respond that conditions
were becoming more equal, that it is in the nature of democracy
to become more democratic, as if equality were the only lasting
goal even if it is always an unfinished goal. He has in mind the
contrast between democracy and aristocracy, between individuals
in motion, rising and falling, and a fixed hierarchy of class
distinctions. To introduce democracy he presents it as a seven-
hundred-year-old trend, dating from the opening of the ranks of
the church's clergy to all, not only to nobles—a hidden trend now
coming to view "in broad daylight" in America, the country where
Tocqueville came to seek "the image of democracy itself."

Yet, unlike liberal theorists, he does not set forth the logic of
the image, even though he says he will explore its "theoretical
consequences." He turns to the actual practice of democracy in its
"point of departure," the coming of the Puritans to America. The
Puritans called themselves pilgrims because they came to America
on behalf of an idea rather than for money or adventure, and the
idea, though primarily religious, was also a political theory of
democracy in which the people are sovereign, ruling all society,
regulating mores, and establishing public education. Democracy
appears not only as equality but as self-government that presides
over a democratic society or "social state." The point of departure
is a certain kind of society, democratic as opposed to aristocratic,
not the state of nature of liberal theory, in which all are individuals
and society does not yet exist.

Democracy is a certain social state that is not very sociable. An
example in America was the change in inheritance law from
primogeniture to equal inheritance or inheritance by choice.
Primogeniture is designed to keep aristocratic landed estates
intact and to nurture family pride in one's forbears, while equal
inheritance releases individual selfishness from family ties and
induces thoughts of the future rather than the past. Equality
penetrates all society, sometimes as a passion for competitive

excellence elevating humble men to the level of the great—a "manly and legitimate passion," Tocqueville calls it—sometimes as a depraved taste for envy, prompting the weak to drag the strong down to their level. Instead of the state of nature producing democracy, as in Hobbes and Locke, democracy produces something like the state of nature, individuals not necessarily in conflict but not strongly bonded with one another.

How are democratic individuals to be strong, not weak? Tocqueville does not say they will necessarily be one or the other. His concept of the "social state" separate from politics sounds like sociology, a science just getting started in his time. But in contrast to sociologists and to other social scientists today, he does not believe that social characteristics determine politics, for to think so ignores the weight of politics on society that he illustrates with the law on inheritance. Does that law come from the social state or determine it? Tocqueville equivocates, for he says that the social state is both a product of fact or law *and* a first cause of most social behavior. The importance of political liberty appears to be at stake: What good is political liberty if politics is the consequence of a certain social state and cannot decide important questions? So, despite saying that the social state may be considered the first cause of its way of life, he proceeds to speak of the sovereignty of the people—implying the importance of who rules but leaving the impression that democracy is ruled by its social state as much as it rules itself.

Tocqueville goes so far as to conclude: "The people reign over the American political world as does God over the universe." The people are "the cause and the end of all things." But if the American people are like God, they would seem to replace God as sovereign. Man, not God, is sovereign, which is a definite change in the Puritan idea that he called the "point of departure." Puritan democracy was a theocracy, and Tocqueville would not be a liberal if he wanted that. Political liberty sets limits to democratic politics, preventing the state from the strict regulation of mores that we today call "Puritan," because it wants democratic individuals to be free. Tocqueville is a champion of the principle of separating church from state. But he endorses the democratic politics that the Puritans brought to America because one is not free unless one rules. In this confusing proportion between man and God, he shows that liberty has both a debt to religion and a claim against it.

The township

Free individuals by themselves are weak, and Tocqueville must explain how they become strong, so that democratic equality results in strengthening them rather than encouraging their envy. What strengthens individuals is association—a key topic in Tocqueville that he approaches through his discussion of the New England township. In aristocracy, individuals are fixed in a hierarchy between those on whom they depend and those who depend on them. Hardly "individuals," they have their associations supplied for them. But in democracy, men are free—or deprived of—these bonds and must make their associations for themselves. To do this they have a natural disposition to associate with other men at their disposal, second only to their self-love—again a contrast to the "state of nature" that conceives individuals to be at war.

Township is both natural and fragile. It is "so much in nature that everywhere men are gathered, a township forms by itself," yet among civilized nations it is found only in America. The reason is that township government is like a "primary school" of freedom, immature and inexpert, which higher authorities are always tempted to interfere with and set right. Only America has the wisdom, or the good luck that Tocqueville has the wisdom to point out, to keep the township intact. Tocqueville calls it a *form* of government because it is orderly, open to view and public; it is government neither hidden nor remote but in broad daylight. The township, to be sure, is authorized by the state governments to which Tocqueville turns next, but he begins his analysis of democracy as a form of government from the bottom up, where it is most spontaneous.

The dogma of the sovereignty of the people says that each individual is "as enlightened, as virtuous, as strong" as anyone else. Yet if he is to accomplish anything beyond his own individual powers, he must associate with others; and if he associates, he must obey those who have been set in charge. Tocqueville uses the English word "selectmen" for those in charge of a township; if he had said it in French, he might have called them the *elite*. Now since each individual is declared equal in capacity to any other person, why should he obey? He obeys not because he is inferior but because it is useful to obey. He swallows his pride for the sake of accomplishing something, such as the building of a road, that he cannot do by himself. And at the end he still has his pride, the pride of accomplishment together with the pleasure of being sociable. He has learned, as if in primary school, that he can obey and still be free. In the introduction to *Democracy in America*, Tocqueville had said that democracy in Europe has been "abandoned to its savage instincts"; here in the American township, it thrives while enjoying the legitimacy it lacks there.

In the township America teaches itself how to live in freedom, and with his analysis Tocqueville teaches America what it is doing. He admits that township government is not found everywhere in America, and he no doubt exaggerates its virtues, urging them with his praise. If the sovereignty of the people worked from the top down instead of from the bottom up, as in France, it would be imposed and would not be felt. Township government, with many elected offices, satisfies many petty ambitions and attaches citizens to their government as their own. It habituates them to the forms of government, "forms without which freedom proceeds only through revolutions." Democracy thrives through elections, and, Tocqueville says, it is not that America has elections because it is prosperous, but it is prosperous because it has elections.

Another form that teaches self-government to Americans is the jury, "a school, free of charge and always open, where each juror comes to be instructed in his rights." In England the jury of one's peers was an aristocratic institution, but in America it is democratized. It teaches citizens how to judge, which means how to execute general laws, of the kind democratic legislatures are eager to pass, in particular circumstances where equity may require some adjustment. It teaches "each man not to recoil from responsibility for his own acts"—a manly political virtue, he says. Tocqueville endows the jury with great power. It is the "most energetic means of making the people reign"—perhaps a deliberate exaggeration to suit his strategy of advising or urging in the guise of praising. And what makes the people reign "is also the most efficacious means of teaching them to reign." In America, a free people learns by doing, not by consulting a theory before acting.

In general, judging moderates the sovereignty of the people, showing them that their sovereignty has limits, that it must be expressed in laws, and that even good laws, when executed, may be too harsh. At the same time the election of judges in American states reveals that in elections generally the people have an arbitrary power of dismissal that cannot be fully justified or remedied. However controlled and moderated the people's sovereignty may be, it retains an element of the irrational. The sovereignty of the people may be finally no more rational than that of a monarch; both have their whims. Freedom cannot be made altogether reasonable, and free citizens who see their party and their candidates lose must learn to accept the people's decision with equanimity.

In view of the political advantages of the township and the jury, Tocqueville makes a distinction concerning centralization in government that is still often cited. Centralization of the government is good if it joins together the force of common interests, but centralized administration in executing government enervates people who submit to it because, by demanding uniformity, it tends to diminish "the spirit of the city" in them, the practice of self-government combined with resistance to outsiders reflected in the local freedom of the township and the jury. He admits that centralized administration may be more efficient, but it feeds on itself, becoming ever more invasive and clumsy, oblivious to the harm it does when it takes administration out of the hands of the people, spurning their free cooperation, and keeps it in bureaucrats who direct it from the center. France is the epitome of this error, as the administration of the monarchy by such ministers as Cardinals Richelieu and Mazarin set a bad example that was followed by the French Revolution. The United States, however, with its federalism, kept local administration alive and followed the good example of administrative decentralization in England—another instance of an institution adapted from aristocracy and democratized.

The system of federalism in America is the union established under the Constitution, and Tocqueville turns from the township, described as a natural and spontaneous form, and from the individual states, also called natural, like a father's authority, to the union, called a "work of art." He delivers an encomium on the constitutional founding of 1787–89, praising the Americans as a "great people warned by its legislators" of a crisis, looking upon itself for a period of two years, sounding the depth of the ill, finding the remedy at leisure, and submitting to it "without its costing humanity one tear or drop of blood." This achievement was "new in the history of societies." In keeping with the principle of the sovereignty of the people, Tocqueville first gives the credit for it to the American people, later praising the founders and the Federalist party for leading the way. He calls them "the finest minds and noblest characters that had ever appeared in the New World." He seems to suggest that sovereignty is sometimes best shown not in assertiveness but in patience and deference to those with superior virtue.

Associations and self-interest

What a sociologist today might call a group Tocqueville calls an
association. The word implies that society is made from associating
oneself with others (the French verb is reflexive). Associating
is natural to humans, if less so than acting on one's own. But in
democracy, all are equal and hence independent of one another; so
the passion for equality tends to individualize citizens. Association
has to be accomplished and cannot be taken for granted.
Tocqueville calls almost any grouping of more than two people an
association: marriage ("the conjugal association"), a private club, a
joint business venture, a political party, a township, a nation, even
the human race. Here is another singular feature of his liberalism.
Whereas John Stuart Mill, a more typical liberal, does his best to
defend the value of individuality in not conforming to majority
opinion, Tocqueville expands on the benefits for liberal society of
associating. He is less confident than Mill that individuals can be
taught to stand up to the majority, and he wants also to persuade
the majority that it need not demand conformity.

Political associations are the first kind he considers, and in the
second volume he adds a distinction between political and civil
associations. These are both informal associations of what he
calls "civil society," a term widely used today to refer to the realm
between the state and the individual. But Tocqueville uses it also
for the township, as well as for the other forms of government.
To associate is, or tends to be, political; it is an act of political
liberty. Tocqueville says that a civil association is one between
those of a similar interest, and a political one is among dissimilars,
but he does not seem to have his heart set on the distinction,
for he actually calls his chief example, the temperance societies
of nineteenth-century America, civil at one point and political
at another. In the United States today such associations as the
National Rifle Association or the American Association of Retired
Persons are composed of people with a similar interest, but are
obviously very political too.

The reason that political and civil associations are not distinct is that Americans learn how to associate from associating in politics. The people schools itself, Tocqueville says, first in regard to the township and the jury, then speaking of associations generally: they are to be considered "great schools, free of charge, where all citizens come to learn the general theory of associations." Now what *is* that general theory? Tocqueville does not define it, but he does refer to both an art and a science of association, somehow combining human action and human understanding in such manner that the theory arises from the actual practice of association.

The theory is such that the people can learn it. Associating is a kind of free schooling because it is relatively painless and does not place unreasonable expectations upon democratic citizens, who are, after all, human beings. Americans expect to put themselves first and do not believe they are required to be selfless. The American (or Anglo-American) doctrine is summed up in Tocqueville's famous formulation, "self-interest well understood"— meaning in the first place a self-interest one must think about. Tocqueville does not say it is his doctrine, but that Americans believe in it.

In noting American reliance on self-interest, Tocqueville differs from much current discussion on democratic participation, sometimes called "communitarian." Communitarian sentiment is opposed to self-interest; it wants to be altruistic and selfless, for the common good as opposed to selfish or market-oriented. For him, sentiment on behalf of the community comes out of one's self-interest and is useful to it rather than selfless and opposed. Today it is also assumed that the only community is a democratic one, community among equals, as in the phrase "democratic participation," but for him there is also aristocratic community, individuals linked in a hierarchy. And democratic community, we have seen in the township, utilizes and gives opportunity to the talents and ambition of unequal individuals while constructing itself out of equal individuals.

Of course, much depends on what is included in the "well understood" (*bien entendu*) part of the formula. It is sometimes translated "rightly understood" as if benefit that is not immediately in one's interest could be rightly understood as self-interest. Or is it better to suppose that self-interest "well understood" needs to be accompanied by things that seem not to be in one's interest, such as honor and virtue?

The issue arises in the discussion of the "necessity of forms" in democracy, a theme throughout the book. In his summary at the end, Tocqueville remarks that democrats "do not readily comprehend the utility of forms; they feel an instinctive disdain for them." Forms or formalities are institutions (with rules and officers) or mores (ceremonies, rituals, courtesies, and "dressing up") or legalities (for example, due process of law) that show respect for others and enable common action with people who are not friends or family. To democrats, these often appear to be mere technicalities, inconveniences that delay or get in the way of the rapid consummation of their desires. They seem fussy and irrational in a democracy, like "standing on ceremony" as if you wanted to appear more or less than you are. But this, for Tocqueville, is precisely their virtue.

Forms place barriers between men, as when formal offices create inequalities between government and people. They place obstacles between men and their desires, when formalities require certain ceremonies or polite manners. They require respect for due process when they compel government to pass a law instead of issuing a decree or acting on a whim. They keep distances among men when they enforce respect for privacy or dignity. Democratic peoples disdain forms because they want to go directly to the object of their desires, preferring action to dignity, sincerity to politeness, result to correctness; in sum, substance to form. Such peoples are naturally impatient by virtue of their equality, which relieves them from having to "behave" and please others more important than they. Self-interest in its primary meaning suits this disposition, as it requires looking at everything for one's advantage, as we say today pragmatically, rather than for its propriety. Yet precisely democratic peoples, who respect forms less, need them more. Their principal merit, says Tocqueville, is to serve as a barrier between the strong and the weak, especially between the government and the governed, forcing the former to slow down and enabling the latter to have time to reflect. Self-interest well understood, for Tocqueville as opposed to his Americans, is to live in a society where one is prevented from going directly to one's self-interest but compelled to do so legally or constitutionally or conventionally or respectfully or formally.

Self-interest, then, both supports associations for their utility and undermines them if they become inconvenient. The readiness to form them is matched by the temptation to ignore or dissolve them. So Tocqueville emphasizes the tumult and agitation "constantly reborn" of political activity in the United States, something he says one cannot understand without having witnessed it there. The activity of associating is especially associating for some new idea or moral purpose, and in America the habit of freedom is even stronger than the love of freedom. In the restive activity and energy of associations the true superiority of democracy to despotism can be found.

Another aspect of self-interest that needs to be "well understood" is the democratic mores (*moeurs*) of Americans. Tocqueville takes for granted the calculation of self-interest in economic activity, but he adds to that the practical experience, habits, and opinions—the mores—that sustain society. Any reader who does not feel the importance he has given to mores, he says, has missed "the principal goal" he proposed to himself in writing his book. Mores were featured in the political philosophy of two eighteenth-century mentors of Tocqueville, Montesquieu and Rousseau, and played a role in the rise of nineteenth-century sociology. Classical political philosophers would have spoken of law in a wide sense (*nomos*), including both written and unwritten laws, but Tocqueville accepts

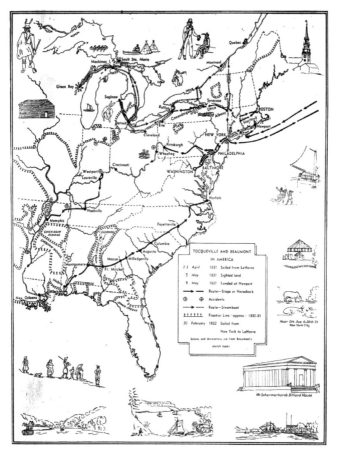

5. Tocqueville and Beaumont's travels in America in 1831–32. Tocqueville was only twenty-five years old when he and Beaumont departed for their nine-month journey.

the liberal distinction between the two. In the liberal theory of Hobbes and Locke, the purpose of the distinction is to elevate laws made by a sovereign and derived from the consent of the people above customs that might hinder the decisions of the sovereign. But for the sake of political liberty Tocqueville wants those sovereign decisions to be not so much hindered as scattered at large in democratic society. In another disagreement with pristine liberal theory he elevates mores above laws, since mores maintain the laws. Laws may sometimes change mores, as a new inheritance law helped to democratize the American family, but mores, "habits of the heart" as well as those of the mind, comprise the "whole moral and intellectual state of a people."

Mores therefore include religion. Is religion a factor in the American doctrine of "self-interest well understood"? The answer: in a complicated way. Tocqueville treats religion in both volumes of *Democracy in America*, but somewhat differently in each. In the first, religion is the root of the mores that help maintain a democratic republic in America. It is considered for this function, not for its truth—and he says that what is most important is not that all citizens profess the true religion, but that they profess a religion. In this political view, religion serves politics, rather than politics serving religion, as with the Puritans. Religion "harmonizes the earth with heaven" by compelling humans to respect insurmountable barriers, "certain primary givens" that restrain their will. Religion sets limits to human sovereignty and therefore to the sovereignty of the people in a democracy. It does this mostly through women rather than men, for democratic men are hardly to be restrained in their desire to become rich, but women make mores, and religion "reigns as a sovereign over the soul of woman."

The weight that Tocqueville assigns to mores in politics, he thus assigns also to women. Paradoxically, one sees in his discussion of women in volume 2 that the condition of women's influence is that they stay out of politics themselves. The same condition applies to the clergy. Tocqueville firmly supports the separation of church and state, and the main reason is that religion loses its concern for the other world when it interferes in the politics of this world. To secure its power, religion must keep its purity—and then, when it stays out of politics, it can have the most power in politics—for the sake of fostering restraint. Both women and the clergy hold their power indirectly, by refraining from exercising it directly. Together religion and the family represent an indispensable nonpolitical supplement to politics that keeps it under restraint with the reminder of a higher and more intimate life than political life. Both religion and family are, however, in a sense political because they are necessary to self-government.

Thomas Jefferson wrote the last letter of his life (on June 4, 1826) about the Declaration of Independence he had authored and in it did not hesitate to insert a swipe at "monkish ignorance and superstition" as the enemy of Enlightenment. For Tocqueville, despotism can do without religious faith, but freedom cannot. Though Americans do not allow religion to mix directly in government, he says, it should be considered as "the first of their political institutions," not so much giving them their taste for freedom as facilitating their use of it. In their minds they "completely confuse Christianity and freedom," a conclusion enabling him to avoid judging how sincerely Christian Americans are. Americans believe religion to be useful, but it would appear to be useful only if they believe in it because it is true, rather than as a political institution. Religion cannot be "well understood" in the manner of self-interest, as if Americans were impiously looking on their religion from outside it in order to conclude that their piety is a good thing.

In this context Tocqueville, leaving Jefferson untouched, inserts a swipe of his own at those in France who condemn Americans for not believing with the atheist philosopher Spinoza in the eternity of the world. In the introduction to *Democracy in America* he had put among the "intellectual miseries" of Europe the parties that set religion and liberty in fierce opposition, and clearly an alliance between the two is the first principle of his new political science and a distinguishing feature of his new liberalism.

Although the religion the Puritans brought from England was democratic and republican, religion in general is "the most precious inheritance from aristocratic centuries." There are a number of aristocratic features of democracy in America that Tocqueville brings to our attention singly. While noting each one, he never adds them up—perhaps because the sum would make aristocracy too conspicuous. For him, aristocracy and democracy are successive eras in history, and aristocracy as a whole, as a principle, has left the scene, gone for good. But if aristocracy is gone for good, it is no longer a danger to democracy. Tocqueville can help us appreciate its virtues and charms without seeming to stand up for its defense. He does not attempt to mix aristocracy with democracy, and he declares resoundingly that the mixed regime is a "chimera" because in every society one always discovers "one principle of action that dominates all others." In rejecting the mixed regime, Tocqueville abandons the central strategy of classical political science and casts doubt on the idea of liberal pluralism. But he retains the idea of mixing holdover aristocratic features into democracy as long as its principle is not challenged.

Democracy and aristocracy are two wholes, each being a way of life driven to make itself absolute, thus constituting "as it were, two distinct humanities." So Tocqueville declares at the end of *Democracy in America*. Yet he wants to moderate the absolute and partisan character of the democratic humanity without challenging the democratic principle of the sovereignty of the people. He leaves it to his readers to sum up the democratic mores and institutions that are said to be aristocratic in origin or character. Besides religion, he mentions the jury, once aristocratic as being judged by one's peers, now democratized. America's devotion to local self-government, to free speech, and to its free press also come from aristocratic England. Democratic associations are artificially created substitutes for the influence of "aristocratic persons," and lawyers with their love of order and of legal formalities comprise a conservative aristocracy within democratic America. The "secondary powers" Tocqueville repeatedly recommends as a cure for democratic centralization are natural to aristocracy, and so are the democratic forms he praises: indeed, the American Constitution was made by the Federalist party and inspired by its "aristocratic passions."

Most striking in this list is Tocqueville's attribution of rights to the English landed aristocracy. The idea of rights was brought over from England not in the political philosophy of John Locke (his name does not occur in the book) but, he says, was taken from the practice of English nobles who stood up to the king, preserving individual rights and local freedoms. In America "freedom is old, equality comparatively new." So in speaking of the practice, mores, and institutions of freedom, he does not introduce rights as the *basis* of practice, as in the Declaration of Independence where men are "endowed by their Creator" with rights prior to the existence of government, but as the practice of self-government itself.

Rights must be exercised with "a political spirit that suggests to each citizen some of the interests that make nobles in aristocracies act." That spirit could remind one of the spiritedness (*thumos*) that Plato and Aristotle describe as bristling like an animal in defense of one's own interests. It is altogether different from economic and social rights guaranteed by government, known today as "entitlements," which are intended to provide security to individuals. For Tocqueville, rights are derived from virtue, from "virtue introduced into the political world." That virtue would prompt one to risk one's security in the defense of liberty—like the signers of the Declaration who mutually pledged their "sacred honor"—or in everyday practice, to abandon the comforts and complacency of political apathy and join an association or run for office.

In using the word "aristocracy," Tocqueville refers to a distinct form of humanity alternative to democracy, but not to the literal sense of the word: "rule of the best." He means a landed aristocracy of noble families. But the aristocratic features of America come from England, and he therefore speaks not only of Americans but frequently of "Anglo-Americans" when he wants to call attention to the continuity—in some regards—between English aristocracy and American democracy. One can say further that Tocqueville's liberalism relies on the nation as well as the social state, rather than the social contract, to describe liberal society. When dwelling on the Anglo-Americans, he says quite pointedly that he will never accept that men form a society merely by recognizing the same head and obeying the same laws— namely, the social contract idea. Instead of that idea, he recounts the actual covenant that the Puritans adopted in God's name and not for the sake of individual self-preservation, as with liberal theory. That America acquired its identity partly from the English stamped it quite differently from what it might have received from another nation and not only in what we today call ethnicity. Its politics and religion, even its philosophy and morals, for example, the notion of self-interest well understood, came to America from England and characterize the dual nation of Anglo-Americans.

What particularly distinguishes the Anglo-Americans from all other peoples is the sentiment of pride, and this is particularly true of Americans, who have "an immense opinion" of themselves. Even their religious zeal "constantly warms itself at the hearth of patriotism," and they send preachers to the frontier as much to improve their country as to save souls. American patriotism is distinct from the England's because it is inspired by democracy rather than the native land and comes out of the exercise of self-government. It is made rather than inherited, and rational, reflective, and enlightened rather than instinctual. For when citizens are active in government as in America, they take credit for the result. They see a connection between their own interest and the common prosperity, and as they work for both, their pride becomes mixed with the desire to become rich. Tocqueville endorses what we now call the American Dream of hard work rewarded, but with emphasis on its basis in politics. American patriotism is "irritable" and annoying to visiting foreigners like Tocqueville, because national pride aggravates and justifies the vanity of each individual so that one is permitted only to praise, never to criticize. It is a consequence of democratic freedom at work, but with significant borrowing from English aristocracy.

Pride is a great feature of Tocqueville's new liberalism. "I would willingly trade several of our small virtues for this vice." He says this against "moralists" who complain against pride, and it applies as well to the formal liberalism of Hobbes, who wants pride or vainglory to be subdued by government, and Locke, who reduces it to a feeling of insecurity or uneasiness. Both thinkers put the right of self-preservation to the fore, declaring that fear for one's life, rather than pride in one's virtue, is the strongest natural desire in humans. For them, and for liberalism in general, pride is the enemy of liberty because it induces the desire to dominate others; and it is contrary to self-interest because a proud person easily becomes hot and fractious, abandoning calculation and charging forward imprudently. Tocqueville disagrees, but he ironically accepts that pride is a vice and adds it to the list of things apparently against one's interest but comprehended in self-interest well understood.

Tocqueville believes that the desire to dominate is not the passion most to be feared in democracy and that the habit of calculating one's interest works more against liberty than for it. In the matter of pride, he shows what he fears as well as what he praises in American democracy. He praises its self-government and the pride of accomplishment by free human beings, giving evidence of their elevation above the rest of nature that merely obeys and cannot rule itself. But he also observes that democracy acts against pride and tends to subdue it, as when a rich man runs for election. The intent of democratic moralists and liberal theory toward this very end has been achieved in great part by democratic society acting on its own and without their advice. Yet in humbling the proud, democracy creates a pride of its own as necessary in its way as the pride of aristocrats in aristocracy.

Because pride is so important to liberty, Tocqueville returns to the soul. Pride means that you are conscious of your self, hence above yourself—one elementary meaning of "soul." The soul can take a view of the self, an approving view in pride, a reproving one in shame. Such a soul introduces, or reintroduces, complication to his notion of human nature. He speaks frequently of the "soul." His new liberalism is liberalism with soul, as it is indebted to the old notion of soul that liberalism tried to replace with the self. The liberal self had an interest in gain that was not complicated by the critical view of a soul above the self. The liberal self was not capable of pride or shame and unlikely to be satisfied; it just wanted more. Tocqueville does not simply return to the classical notion of an orderly soul, but he invokes the classical and Christian notion of an elevated soul.

Thus the main fear Tocqueville expresses in the introduction to *Democracy in America* is that democracy as seen in Europe degrades souls. Aristocracy, he says, was based on the belief that the nobles' privileges were the immutable order of nature, an illusion to be sure, but considered legitimate by the people who had to obey. Democracy, however, has not established legitimate institutions there to replace aristocratic privileges that have been overturned, and the people, though no longer "serfs," obey existing powers out of fear rather than love and respect. Obedience from fear is acting out of urgent necessity, which degrades the soul because the people feel the shame of their base surrender to authority, even to democratic authority, and cannot respect themselves or think themselves free.

The cause of this depressing condition is not so much moral faults as certain "intellectual miseries" in the present landscape of Europe. These same errors are at work in the actual democracy in America, where citizens feel proud and believe their government to be legitimate and their obedience to it reasonable.

Chapter 3
Informal democracy

Tocqueville approves of the formal democracy in America that gives effect to the sovereignty of the people. He praises the constitutional forms, conceived in all their calculated complexity by its founders, the simple, spontaneous form of the township brought to America by the Puritans, and the art of association that underlies them. These forms enable the people to govern themselves effectively and, as a result, to live sensibly and prosper economically. They make political liberty possible because they *are* political liberty, which is liberty in practice, not merely in theory. In governing themselves, the American people feel the pride that goes with being free, while making a success of democracy.

Majority power

Yet Tocqueville sees there is an informal democracy more powerful than the formal one. Forms of association provide structure—both hierarchy and procedure—that enable people to work together—but these channels or enabling devices are also barriers that delay or obstacles that prevent the will of the people from getting its way immediately. They can bring frustrated, impatient pride instead of pride in accomplishment. In the second part of the first volume of *Democracy in America*, Tocqueville announces a shift in his presentation from the principle or dogma of the sovereignty of the people (announced in chapter 4 of the first part) to its actual governing. The second part begins with the chapter title "How one can say strictly that in the United States the people govern." He declares that "the opinions, the prejudices, the interests, and even the passions of the people" have "no lasting obstacles" to their will. The people govern through a representative form of government, but they choose their representatives frequently, direct them, and keep them dependent. Moreover, "the people" refers not to a formal body never acting but to the majority that rules in their name.

Informal democracy is just what the old, formal liberalism tried to forestall with the ideas of representation and separation of powers. Hobbes and Locke conceived of a formal democracy in the state of nature, but it had only a fleeting existence, if that, and its purpose was to legitimize a sovereign that would govern in the name of—that is, instead of—the people. Locke and Montesquieu, seeing that the people's representatives might be unfaithful, worked out a formal separation of powers that would compel the government to check itself. And *The Federalist* perfected these two fundamental forms of free government, so that the American Constitution was entirely representative in every branch and the separated powers were set in a new, improved balance, together with a newly invented federalism. These measures were carefully designed to "refine and enlarge" the people's will through elections, and if that did not happen, to provide "auxiliary precautions" to deal with a runaway government or an unruly people, installing the reason of the people to regulate its passions.

Tocqueville disagrees, and his "new kind" of liberalism abandons the hope of the old liberalism that a democratic beginning, in the state of nature, can avoid a democratic conclusion in the government that results. Liberal forms designed to keep the sovereign people under discipline will simply be overrun. To say that there will be no *lasting* obstacle to the people's will implies that immediate whims may be curtailed... but maybe not. It is an idea closer to Rousseau (one of Tocqueville's acknowledged masters) than to the liberals whom Rousseau also criticized for their sophisticated stratagem of having the people be represented instead of ruled. But Tocqueville did not accept, and did not allude to, Rousseau's proposal to substitute a new form of the social contract for liberal representative government. Whatever forms theorists offer, the democratic people will eventually do what it wants.

Having asserted that the people strictly rule, Tocqueville moves to the informal instruments of its rule, and first to political parties. Parties are not properly speaking about ethnic identity (as we would say) but divisions over common interests affecting all groups equally. They are an evil inherent in free governments, he says, agreeing with the traditional disesteem for them, and they may be divided into great parties, parties of principle like the Federalists and the Jeffersonians, and small parties without ideas that are concerned only with holding office. Yet even small parties such as the Jacksonian Democrats at the time of Tocqueville's visit to America have "secret instincts" that refer to the two great parties to be found in all free societies—the democratic instinct for extending the power of the people, and the aristocratic desire to restrain them. Informally, even in democracy, where the people are sovereign, there is a party that wants to restrict them, as if aristocracy even when discordant were irrepressible in human nature.

The free press in America is a weapon of its parties and also an informal factor in the sovereignty of the people. Government by the people is government by their opinions, which they choose: the power of the press is to formulate the opinions that the people choose. This is the power of the enlightened, but in the United States there is no intellectual capital equivalent to Paris, and the enlightened are dispersed so that they cannot readily address the whole nation. The spirit of the journalist in America by contrast to France, where he has more power, is one of coarse attack, appeal to passion, avoidance of principle, and scandalous revelations.

In sum, a free press is a mixture of goods and evils that has to be accepted as such, there being no tenable middle between a press completely free and one silenced and enslaved.

Another feature of informal democracy, also a mix of good and bad, is the political association. Americans enjoy an extreme freedom of political association that is considered dangerous even among liberals in Europe. Yet it sometimes happens, Tocqueville says, that extreme freedom can correct the abuses of freedom. This does happen in America, where there is great tolerance of opposition, as in the nullification crisis of 1831 to which he alludes. But such action comes often at the cost of sacrificing independence of thinking within the association as it seeks a united front. Such associations do good because by seeking change they "weaken the moral empire of the majority," yet by seeking the consent of the majority they also endorse its moral force. The sovereignty of the people implies the equal capacity of each and the moral force of all, but in fact it is the rule of the majority over each in the name of all.

Majority tyranny

Tocqueville makes his way carefully in this part of *Democracy in America*, as if he wants to break the news in stages. He had spoken about tyranny in the first part of the first volume, where he praises American forms of government, but never in regard to the majority. The phrase "tyranny of the majority" appears in the chapter on political associations, then is featured in the title of the seventh chapter on the "omnipotence" of the majority, which in the body of the chapter comes out as the "tyranny" of the majority and finally as a new "despotism." This is the specter behind the sovereignty of the people, which, up to this point, had been developed and praised.

Omnipotence, Tocqueville says, is safe with God, because His wisdom and justice are equal to His power. But with imperfect human beings this is not the case. Omnipotence in the human sovereign brings tyranny, not necessarily but probably, unless there is a guarantee against it. Tocqueville does not want his sovereign people to take over God's sovereignty intact as proposed in the liberal principles of Hobbes, Spinoza, and Locke.

But what is the guarantee against the majority in the United States? Public opinion forms the majority; the legislature represents and obeys the majority; so does the executive; the military is the majority under arms; the jury is the majority issuing decrees. The rule of law is no guarantee against majority tyranny, as Tocqueville shows explicitly in his phrase "the tyranny of the laws." He defines tyranny as rule against the interest of the ruled, as distinct from arbitrariness without law. So law can be an instrument of majority tyranny, and arbitrary rule can be used in the interest of the ruled, though if it is absolute it is not likely to be. Tyranny is one-man rule, except that when a majority acts tyrannically, it thinks and moves as one man. In America, the majority is flattered by its courtiers and "lives in perpetual adoration of itself," just like Louis XIV.

Majority tyranny has a new character under democracy. Under monarchy ("the absolute government of one alone") despotism would strike the victim's body in order to reach his soul, but democratic despotism "leaves the body and goes straight for the soul." Democratic despotism, to use Tocqueville's phrase in volume 2 of *Democracy in America*, is "mild despotism," not torture and execution but moral and intellectual domination, not hard but soft. Yet it is not all soft. In a footnote Tocqueville gives two examples of majority tyranny: in Baltimore, two journalists who opposed the War of 1812 were killed by a mob of the war's supporters, and in Philadelphia, black freedmen were kept from voting by intimidation. The second example of racial discrimination Tocqueville takes up at length in a remarkable chapter on the three races—white, black, and Indian—in America.

This chapter, the last in the first volume of *Democracy in America*, and the culmination of its treatment of the sovereignty of the people, is by far the longest. The subjects covered are particularly American, Tocqueville says, dealing with the three races in connection with the future of America. But his deeper intent is to reveal the nature of majority tyranny and what can be done to prevent it, by way of an analysis of pride and freedom.

The two most offensive instances of majority tyranny in America were, and still are, the virtual extermination of the Indians and the enslavement of blacks. Tocqueville studies the three races, not merely the two subject races, because he wants to show the effects of tyranny on the tyrant as well as on the victims. Tyranny, defined as "not in the interest of the governed," emerges in modern peoples especially because they have been taught to believe in the omnipotence of man rather than God, "the right and the ability to do everything."

Tocqueville says nothing about the natural or inherent superiority of a race. Rather, the three races are distinguished by the pride they show, or the lack of it. The white or Anglo-American in the New World Tocqueville calls "man par excellence," for he treats other races as a man would treat a beast, man over nature. He tyrannizes two subject races, which hold two opposite extremes. The Indian in his barbarous independence represents the extreme limit of both pride and freedom, and the black is kept down in the opposite extreme of servile imitation and slavery. The behavior of the two subject races is quite contrary: the black accepts white civilization and tries to join white society, which rejects and repels him, while the Indian, proud of his ancestry and confident of the bounty of nature, refuses white civilization and remains aloof. The Indian knows freedom, but because he lives under the illusions of his nobility, he cannot control himself and cannot preserve himself. The black knows how to preserve himself but cannot find dignity in being the possession of another man, so cannot improve himself and be free. Each extreme situation reveals the result of majority tyranny as an abuse of pride: too much pride brings the fate of the inflexible Indian, too little brings the subjection of the black. Without a due concern for pride the white majority could suffer the same calamitous misfortune it imposes on its victims. Reason needs to be linked with pride in order to produce freedom, for in democracy it can always seem reasonable to trade freedom for administrative efficiency. But pride needs reason to temper its illusions and to bring it to submit to civilization. To civilization, Tocqueville makes clear, not merely to expertise.

In endorsing pride, Tocqueville again differs from liberalism in the original form laid down by Thomas Hobbes. His theory claims that men must not merely temper but renounce their pride in order to produce civilization. In the state of nature men live in a state of war, a war of all against all, and in that state the

6. A sketch by Tocqueville's friend and traveling companion Gustave de Beaumont, of himself and Tocqueville (reclining against the fallen tree), along with an Indian guide who led them through the wilderness in Michigan.

illusions of their vanity need to be plunged into a cold bath of fear for their self-preservation. After this experience, either in fact or imagination, men are ready to be civil and accommodating, if not servile, to their fellows in civilized society. For Hobbes and his many followers, freedom and pride are in conflict, and the lesson is that civilized men must learn to be sensitive and get along.

Tocqueville takes a course opposed to this, displayed in this same chapter. Instead of a social contract constituting a trade-off of pride for civilization, he wants to retain human pride as being inseparable from human freedom. The Indian with his primitive freedom must be combined with the black and his willingness to be civilized. The result would be a "white" who preserves his freedom because he keeps his pride and who preserves himself because his dignity is not based on illusion. Of course such a "white" would not have to be racially white, but whites as they are would have to renounce their prejudice against the two subject races—which Tocqueville does not think likely.

When slavery is allied with race, as in America and in modern slavery generally, the slave is marked forever by his color. The prejudice of the white sees him as inferior in humanity, somewhere between a man and a beast. Liberals may assert—and the Declaration of Independence may declare—that all men are created equal, but the claim actually makes slavery more difficult to abolish because the whites do not see blacks to be fully human. A despot could abolish slavery in America, as the European powers abolished it in their colonies.

Democratic Americans, however, take pride in the equality of whites only, while at the same time (even in the North) they fear revolt from the slaves. The racial pride they show is not understood by liberal theory, which glosses over the question of race, and the fear they reveal works against racial equality instead of in its favor, as supposed by liberal theory. The proud behavior of the Indians, rejecting the ways of whites, shows that liberal theory takes the attraction of civilization for granted and does not understand that one must submit to it. The prejudice of whites, rejecting the blacks, shows that, despite the penchant of democracy contrary to pride, pride does not disappear and must be dealt with, and wholesome objects found for it. The pride many Americans reveal in their prejudice must be turned to the advantage of pride in the freedom of self-government. One cannot merely equalize all pretensions in the state of nature and proceed to a social contract, as liberals often presume in their theories.

Tocqueville agrees with liberal theory that slavery is unnatural, but not because we all begin equally free in the state of nature. Indignantly he exclaims that in slavery we see "the order of nature reversed." Yet in another sense of nature, it was all too natural for Europeans to enslave a different race they perceived as inferior—it was understandable. The order of nature is for the best, but the best is not achieved automatically; indeed it faces obstacles from the pride natural to humans. Liberal theory believes it has conquered pride in the state of nature, and it aligns the order of nature (natural law) with the most powerful human passion, fear for one's self-preservation. For Tocqueville this is an elegant but too simple solution. His thought on democracy is absorbed with pride, and he focuses not merely on opposing prejudice and abandoning false pride, as we do so readily today, but rather on the more difficult task of finding a remedy for *lack* of pride. Democracy is uncomfortable with the pretensions of pride, which always imply some sort of inequality, but it needs the pride to be found in its own sense of importance and accomplishment as seen especially in its politics.

Almost immediately after introducing majority tyranny, Tocqueville speaks of the "power that the majority exercises over thought." He makes the flat statement that "I do not know any country where, in general, less independence of mind and genuine freedom of discussion reign than in America." It is not that a dissident need fear being persecuted or burned at the stake, but that *nobody will listen*, and he will be dismissed from consideration, finally shushed. This is an "intellectual" violence that closes the mind and, more effectually than the Inquisition, takes away from authors even the thought of publishing views contrary to the majority's opinion. Tocqueville cites as evidence the fact that "America has not yet had great writers."

Of course Tocqueville's own book was translated and published in America soon after it appeared in France, apparently regardless of the majority's opinion. But several times in the book he shows himself wary of being thought hostile either to America or to democracy, and particularly at the beginning of volume 2, where he declares his unwillingness to flatter either the great parties or the little factions of his time. Moreover, a modern reader might respond that America's great writers, such as they are, were soon to appear: Nathaniel Hawthorne's *Scarlet Letter* in 1850, Herman Melville's *Moby-Dick* in 1851, to mention only two. James Fenimore Cooper's *The Last of the Mohicans* (1826) came out in time for Tocqueville's consideration in this judgment. Still, one would not want to run afoul of his stricture against Americans, none of whom, he says, can stand the least criticism of their country.

In the chapter on freedom of the press, Tocqueville remarks that there are three kinds of opinion: belief, doubt, and rational conviction. The last is achieved by very few; most people live in belief, during ages of religion, or in doubt, in the democratic age. Here is one of his brilliant paradoxes: he says that in times of belief, people will change their opinions when they are converted, but in times of doubt they hold to their opinions. Why the latter? When men doubt, they see no better opinion than their own and feel no closer interest, which is likely to be a material interest easily compatible with stubbornness, prejudice, and fixity of opinion.

A free press, therefore, does not induce people to live by rational conviction or by truth. Claims made today for the press that the people have a right to know are too lofty. Most people do not live on the basis of knowledge but of complacent opinion. They are skeptical: "You can't believe what you read!" And we say today that the media always get it wrong. Consequently we believe that we are right, there being no authority above us to say we are wrong. Democrats like to pride themselves on independence of thought, which is just the kind of independence they display the least. Tocqueville identifies two hidden advantages of a free press: employment for the ambition of talented writers using their vulgar cleverness against one another, and stability of opinion engendered by the very confusion that enables people to distrust or dismiss what they are told.

In volume 2 Tocqueville addresses the authority of science, which attempts to produce rational conviction of a sort in the people, halfway between full knowledge and uninformed opinion. But in this discussion he lays stress on both the "inestimable good" that a free press provides and the irrational self-indulgence of the majority that it nourishes in the name of enlightenment. With characteristic moderation he measures it against both a regime of censorship, a usual contrast for liberals, and reason in the highest sense, not so usual. The result is quite a different picture from the paean to "liberty of thought and discussion" to be found in John Stuart Mill's *On Liberty*, published in 1859, the year of Tocqueville's death.

Mill was a friend and, as reviewer of *Democracy in America*, an early patron of Tocqueville, but they differed deeply in their view of the relationship between reason and pride. Mill believed that the prejudice of ordinary people could be overcome by persons now called "intellectuals," who could direct society without actually governing it; he regarded human pride as an impediment and political liberty as an instrument of progress in knowledge. Tocqueville sees pride as both good and bad for democracy, bad when it enthrones the prejudice of a democratic majority, good when it helps to correct that prejudice in the "free school" that political liberty provides. For him, the highest reason represents "the last refuge" of human pride, and though theoretical discoveries may lead to social improvement, they must be undertaken for their own sake. Humans are distinct from animals by their reason; this is the reasonable basis of pride and must be respected in those who are capable of the highest reason. But most humans use their reason, most of the time, to take pride in defending their prejudices. Spreading prejudice is the occupation and calling of a free press.

Equality and similarity

Behind informal institutions is the informal sovereignty of public opinion. In this Tocqueville agrees with Mill, but he is far less optimistic. Mill believed that public opinion could be led by intellectuals like himself, exuding enlightenment, but Tocqueville, while agreeing that the few are more enlightened than the many, thought it more likely that intellectuals would be led by public opinion than lead it. They would not be listened to if they tried to lecture and exhort in the manner of Mill; they would be compelled to serve public opinion. Democratic intellectuals such as Mill tend to be more democratic than the democratic people, while reserving an exception for themselves as instructors of the people. True, Tocqueville himself seeks to "instruct democracy," as he says in the introduction to *Democracy in America*. But he does so through candid analysis of its virtues and faults, mixed with muted praise, rather than by arguing for democracy and blaming its opponents. Without indignation he calmly contrasts democracy with aristocracy.

Public opinion has greater power in democracy than in aristocracy because in the former all are equal or thought equal. No individual or group has more authority than the people, so no one can stand up visibly against them, as happens easily in an aristocracy. The rule of public opinion is in accord with the democratic social state, the Tocquevillean concept that is both prior to politics and determined by politics. Though public opinion in fact rules in a democracy, it does not *seem* to rule because it has no identifiable representative to whom one must listen. It is, to be sure, formed by intellectuals, politicians, and journalists, but since all claim to follow it, no one takes responsibility for it. When public opinion changes, replacing favor with disfavor or vice versa, it does so without explanation, as it is not accountable to anyone. Some may try to interpret public opinion, but public opinion will not say whether they are correct. Its sovereign decisions are not subject to reason, and one cannot object to them that they are inconsistent or short-sighted. Public opinion will be heard but will not listen when it does not wish to.

Democratic public opinion rests on equality, but the nature of this equality needs to be considered. How does democracy deal with obvious natural inequalities? In a democracy each person thinks himself equal to everyone else. The thought of equality is more powerful than the fact of inequality because it can create equality when it does not find it. Your neighbor may be richer than you, but if you think of him as your equal, that is what he becomes. Tocqueville uses the notion of one's similars (*semblables*), or those like oneself, to denote the creative power of democratic public opinion. Your neighbor is not exactly your equal but is someone like you, despite being more or less rich or beautiful or intelligent. Therefore you can treat him as equal, which means that his inequalities do not confer any authority on either him or you.

One must apply the notion of *semblable* to Tocqueville's statement that the democratic revolution is bringing greater equality of condition, a statement some readers object to because it seems to overlook obvious inequalities that continue in what we call "democracy." But what we *call* democracy *is* democracy. Democracy is the rule of equals and unequals, both considering themselves similar to one another. People perceived equal are equal in fact as opposed to equal in the abstract, an equality seen rarely if ever, and conceived by liberal theorists as the state of nature. Tocqueville replaces the so-called natural equality of man with the conventional equality of those who think all others are like themselves. Yet the conventional equality of similars is not simply arbitrary; it stands on the basis of the pride in human nature, by which each thinks himself important. For one can feel proud in having no superior (democracy) as well as proud in being superior (aristocracy).

When you bow to public opinion, you are not bowing to a particular person or group that might seem to be in authority over you. The vagueness of public opinion not only protects it from being accused or held accountable but also permits it to be an authority without feeling like one. Similarity in a democratic people makes democracy feel natural even though it is in good part conventional. While accepting the distinction between human nature and human convention, Tocqueville does not try to sharpen it in the manner of liberal theory, opposing the two as if they were hostile to each other, but instead he blends what is given with what is made.

Pride is both flattered and humiliated in the working of democratic public opinion. When one individual compares himself to another, he feels proud that he is the equal of each, but then when he compares himself to "the sum of those like him," a vast body of people, he is overcome by the sensation of his own insignificance. Thus general opinion "puts an immense weight on the mind of each individual," enveloping, directing, and oppressing him. The more people resemble one another, the weaker one person feels in face of all the others. He begins to distrust himself when he finds himself in disagreement with the majority, so that the majority "does not need to constrain him: it convinces him." That is why great revolutions are rare in democracy, Tocqueville says. Democratic peoples have neither the time nor the taste to seek out new opinions; they stay with the familiar despite its faults regardless of the humiliation they suffer because they are subject to the majority.

Material well-being

Beneath public opinion is the taste for "material well-being," as Tocqueville calls it. The first time he uses the phrase he speaks of its influence on political opinions, particularly visible in foreigners who come to America and prosper. A fellow Frenchman he met on his journey had been an ardent leveler of wealth in France but had learned from his success in America, his opinions changing with his change in fortune and himself no longer a leveler, to discourse on the right of property like an economist or a materialist: Tocqueville brings up the connection—which might seem to be a stretch—between the philosophical doctrine of materialism and the popular taste for material well-being. Both doctrine and taste have an informal power in America, making for a charmless soft mediocrity in several phases of democratic life. He devotes a sequence of seven chapters in volume 2 to the taste, but already in the introduction to volume 1 he had harshly condemned the doctrine, and those who would "make man into matter," as insolent, usurping, and unworthy.

It would seem from the unnamed Frenchman's example that the taste for material well-being in America causes the doctrine in its favor—so that economic opinion is determined by economic interest or class, as in Marxism. But Tocqueville does not take this path. He maintains that the taste for material well-being (in volume 2 also called "material enjoyments") arises out of democracy. It has a political rather than an economic cause, and does not come from capitalism or the spirit of capitalism as Max Weber holds. What is this taste? Tocqueville discusses its character and also connects it to its apparent opposite, the soul—for there is something immaterial about material well-being in American democracy. The democratic soul has its own restive nature derived from the taste for that very thing.

Americans do indeed have a taste for material things, arising from their exceptional situation, that will not be found in all democratic nations, and Tocqueville uses the occasion to deny that America will be the model for them to imitate. America is so extreme in this taste that one must go there to see the power it exerts—this being the second thing, after its facility in making associations, that Tocqueville says one must witness to appreciate. In discussing the three races he says that the northern white has material well-being for the principal goal of his existence, which shows that it is not uniformly dominant. Yet despite these qualifications, he asserts that equality, by some "secret force," makes the passion (not just a taste) for material enjoyments and "the exclusive love of the present" that goes with the passion predominate in the human heart.

What is the secret force? In the chapter on the taste for material well-being in volume 2, Tocqueville again compares democracy with aristocracy. The aristocrat disdains material well-being and can do without necessities, while the democrat can hardly survive without well-being. In our time one could think of modern plumbing, considered a necessity in all democracies. Material well-being is in the middle between rich and poor; the poor want it, the rich are not too proud to insist on it; it spreads with the growth of the middle class. It requires effort to achieve and is indulged only with anxiety. It is a tenacious, exclusive, universal passion, but it has petty aims to which the soul cleaves. Though it prompts democratic peoples to excesses, it is restrained, and Tocqueville says that he reproaches equality not for carrying away men in pursuit of forbidden enjoyments but rather for absorbing them entirely in the search for permitted enjoyments. "They fall into softness rather than debauchery." The taste for material well-being is honest and decent, but only because it lacks great ambition: "It is as difficult to escape the common rule by one's vices as by one's virtues."

A decent desire to acquire the goods of this world is the dominant passion in America, but not the only passion. Tocqueville suddenly brings up a discussion of the soul in this context, at once counteracting the dominant passion and explaining its secret force. Gazing at the picture he draws of itinerant preachers who find their congregations in the wilderness of the West and bring to them an "exalted spiritualism" not seen in Europe, he discloses a truth of human nature. Man, he says, has a taste for the infinite and a love of the immortal. These sublime instincts are not creations of his will but anchored in the immovable foundations of his nature, and they can be hindered or distorted but not destroyed. The soul is not satisfied with enjoyments from the senses; it has needs of its own that must be satisfied and that cannot be distracted for long before it becomes bored, restive, and agitated. The American is restive or restless (*inquiet*) in a manner reminding of the philosophy of Pascal, one of Tocqueville's heroes.

What does this mean for the American doctrine of self-interest well understood? In speaking of the love of the immortal in human nature, Tocqueville implies that one cannot understand everything as coming from the self. Nature is the source of this love, and nature, not man, has made the self. Moreover, love of the immortal seems even to be an extension of the dominant passion, for the desire to acquire becomes the love of the immortal when out of dissatisfaction with the material, it breaks the "narrow fetters that the body wants to impose." Thus material interests are moved by the greater strength of what he wants to call "immaterial interests of man," an impressive expansion of the "well understood" in self-interest. Self-interest in this capacious sense is bound to the self by "material bonds," the human context, but its immaterial truth is above the self. Even Americans implicitly acknowledge that their passion for material things cannot satisfy them—though the experience of transcending materialism may be confined to a few individuals. The soul has needs Americans do not understand, and so when the soul breaks away from material interests, it meets no limits and surges beyond common sense to infinity.

Equality turns men to material goods because it overturns any aristocratic authority above them that would lead or compel them to turn their imaginations to the future and to sacrifice their material interests for a long-term goal. Democrats live in the short term; they have their minds on the present. And what is in the present, visible to all without need for instruction or sacrifice? Material goods. The trouble is that the material goods one acquires increase the thirst for more, bringing discontent rather than satisfaction. In a democracy one is free to change one's place, one's job, one's home, and since Americans set their hearts on the good things of this world, and always more of them, they must always be on the move and in a hurry. No law or custom keeps them where they are. So Americans are grave and sad; they cannot have what they want; life is too short, there are too many choices.

Americans, it is true, unite their taste for material well-being with love of liberty and concern for public affairs, but there is no necessary connection between them. It will often be inconvenient to exercise your political rights, so that self-interest can lead you to neglect your chief interest in this world, which is to remain your own master within the sovereignty of the people. The quest for prosperity is legitimate, but when it causes man to lose "the use of his most sublime faculties," then by wishing to improve everything around him, he degrades himself. "The peril is there, not elsewhere."

Tocqueville accompanies this editorial with a discussion of the doctrine of materialism. Materialism, he says, is a "dangerous malady of the human mind in all nations," but particularly in a democratic people because it combines with its "most familiar vice of the heart." In itself materialism is not democratic, and of course there were materialists in ages of aristocracy. All materialists offend him, as he finds the doctrine pernicious and the materialists themselves revolting in their pride. The doctrine teaches men not to care for politics and morals, even though modern materialism accompanies democracy. One might try to draw from materialism a specious moral lesson telling men that since human matter is no better than other matter, a man should hold a modest idea of himself. But instead, materialists take inordinate pride in declaring that men are nothing more than brutes, acting "as proud as if they had demonstrated they were gods."

The essence of the lawgiver's art, Tocqueville says, is to appreciate the characteristic bent of human societies so as to see where to support the efforts of citizens and where to hold them back. In a democracy, lawgivers and all honest and enlightened men should elevate the souls of their fellow-citizens and turn their attention toward heaven, as they do in America. They should do their best to make spiritualist opinions reign, but to do so is not easy. Socrates and Plato triumphed over the ancient materialists, and their fame, even the survival of their writings in contrast to the mere fragments handed down from the ancient materialists, is owed to the admiration men have for the immaterial part of man. This is not a proof of the truth of spiritualism, and it does seem on the basis of Tocqueville's account that spiritualism would best prove its own truth through the fact that people believe in its truth, that is, through an account of human nature and its aspiration to life or the goal of life beyond the material—to the spiritual.

Now the only simple, general, practical means of teaching man that he has a special value and a special responsibility is to teach him that he has a soul and in particular that the soul is immortal. This means to teach religion. But as a liberal Tocqueville wants only to elevate religion and to hold its spiritualism in honor, and not to establish an official philosophy or church. When the church becomes political, it acquires worldly interests and loses its moral power, hence its political power too. To maintain Christianity, Tocqueville says memorably, "I would rather chain priests in the sanctuary than allow them to leave it." The result in democracy is dispute or conflict between the desire for material enjoyments and religion. The dispute is one that Tocqueville wishes to keep alive because it arises from the human heart, which has room for both a "taste for the goods of the earth and a love of those of Heaven." The human heart spans the distinction between democracy and aristocracy, and provides the ground for Tocqueville's animus against materialism in democracy.

Chapter 4
Democratic despotism

The greatest danger to democracy comes out of democracy. To see it one must return to the most striking difference between the two volumes of *Democracy in America*. After discussing the sovereignty of the people in volume 1, Tocqueville changes his outlook noticeably in volume 2. Instead of the people's sovereignty he tells of a new "individualism" that overturns their conscious sense of governing themselves and installs the "immense being" of big government; instead of majority tyranny, he describes a new "mild despotism" resulting from that government. To give evidence of the change: he does not use the phrase "mild despotism" in volume 1, and no longer refers to "tyranny of the majority" in volume 2. In substance, the change is from conceiving the main danger in democracy as a majority tyranny of active oppression, illustrated in enslavement of blacks, to a mild despotism in which the majority passively surrenders the willful, restive, proud nature characteristic of a tyrant and becomes a "herd of timid and industrious animals."

With this change of words and meaning in view, some scholars have gone so far as to claim that the two volumes are about "two democracies" distinct from each other, and it has become common practice to refer to the first as the 1835 *Democracy* and the second as the 1840 *Democracy*. Perhaps this goes too far. Certainly Tocqueville had time for second thoughts in the five years intervening between the two volumes. Admitting some difference, he says in a letter that the first volume is more about America, the arena of democracy; the second more about democracy itself—but this describes a change of focus rather than opinion. More authoritatively, he says in the "Notice" at the beginning of the second volume that "the two parts [volumes] complete one another and form a single work."

With this express denial, not of a difference, but of an incontinuity in the two volumes, Tocqueville leaves it to his readers to notice the change and to make sense of it on their own. When describing majority tyranny in volume 1 he had already said that the worst of it was tyranny over the mind, not over the body. Perhaps the new democratic despotism is a deliberate development in his argument out of informal democracy rather than a complete change of outlook.

Tocqueville says further in the Notice that he had spoken in the first volume of laws and political mores, and now in the second will discuss "civil society," which means sentiments, opinions, and relations not directly political. Ultimately they are also political, however, and so in the fourth part of volume 2 he returns to describe their influence on democratic politics. Democracy is not only the forms of government and the social state of the American people described in volume 1, but also the way of life, the end of society. Volume 2 shows how democracy looks with respect to its end or aim. Now Tocqueville says, as he had not quite said before, that he is neither an adversary nor a fawning friend to democracy and will therefore speak sincerely. His main target is not its aristocratic enemies, whom he has dismissed as obsolete, but its unwise friends, considered especially in the first part of volume 2, on the democratic intellect.

The democratic intellect

Tocqueville, it has been emphasized, presents American democracy in its practice, as learning by doing and not through philosophical ideas. But in the first part of volume 2, he turns to philosophy to consider not the influence of philosophy on democracy but of democracy on philosophy, on "intellectual movement in the United States." This is an early instance of the phrase "intellectual movement," perhaps the first, and he uses it in the singular, not "movements" in the plural as we would today, to indicate that he wants to see how—and if—the democratic mind works. He has said that democracy is "irresistible," meaning not to be resisted, but it turns out that there are alleged "friends" of democracy who use the word differently. They believe that human beings have no choice but to submit to large, impersonal forces that determine their lives and rob them of the possibility of voluntary, mindful ("intellectual") movement toward the goal of democratic liberty.

Who are they? Tocqueville describes two types of intellectual he regards as harmful, pantheists and democratic historians. But at the beginning of his discussion he singles out one individual, the seventeenth-century French philosopher René Descartes, for special treatment. Americans, he says, give less attention to philosophy than anywhere else in the civilized world, yet all of them use one uniform method for intellectual inquiries, which is to rely on individual effort and judgment, the very method of Descartes. It is in America that his precepts are "least studied and best followed." Its democratic social state both alienates them from philosophy and inclines them to adopt his maxims. In that state men do not hold to tradition, nor do they accept the opinion of a class; seeing no superior to themselves, they come to trust only themselves.

Here is a strange view of Descartes, not usually considered a political philosopher and surely not a democrat, now declared by Tocqueville to be the author, without intending it, of the democratic "method" (Descartes's own term). Here too is a strange view of Americans in thrall to, or living in unconscious agreement with, a French philosopher none of them have ever read. Descartes, whose most famous teaching is to question authority, is himself an authority in America in all but name. His attack on authority has become an authority justifying the sovereignty of the individual. It is hard to say whether Tocqueville has made Descartes or his ignorant American fellow-thinkers more ridiculous. Descartes's philosophy of "clear and distinct ideas" boils down to the clumsy sovereignty of each nonphilosophical American, who knows essentially what he knows without needing to read him. Yet the Americans absurdly place an authority in the people who, if they were following Descartes, should have been consumed with doubt. With such vulgarization and contradiction, what kind of intellectual movement is this?

To explain the democratic mind, Tocqueville reflects on the nature of the human condition. All intellectual, as opposed to instinctual or spontaneous, movement requires the use of one's own mind. To use one's mind means doubting the authority of what one is told. Yet if thinking is to produce action, one must stifle one's doubts. No individual has the time or ability to think through everything for himself, and no society could survive without common action and common ideas. Even the philosopher has to make assumptions, as no one can think about everything at once.

From the need for authority Tocqueville makes an easy transition to the need for belief, as both society and individual must accept a "first foundation" on faith, in truth a kind of enslavement, but a necessary "salutary servitude." Both Descartes and the democratic social state that replicates his philosophy exaggerate the power of human reason. Reason cannot replace authority and establish the autonomy of the individual. All human reason can do is to change aristocratic authority into democratic authority—but it can do this. Man is not by nature "perfectly free," beginning from a condition where there is no authority, as Hobbes and Locke supposed. Democracy is not created from the state of nature in which there is no authority, but rather by democrats who deny the authority of anyone or any class above themselves. In doing so each feels the pride of being equal to every other individual. Yet each is overwhelmed at the same time with a sense of weakness and insignificance in comparison to the "great body" of all other individuals. Democratic authority, therefore, has two opposite effects on the mind: bringing the mind to new thoughts in the denial of tradition and custom and at the same time inducing it to give up thinking in the face of public opinion.

From the need for belief, Tocqueville remarks that the democratic mind loves to generalize. This is a weakness, he thinks. God, who sees both similarities and differences, has no need of general ideas, but man needs the convenience of gathering like objects under the same form. Americans show more interest in general ideas than do their "English forefathers," who represent America's aristocratic past in England as distinct from its democratic point of departure in the Puritans who opposed English aristocracy. Aristocrats have an instinctive distaste for generalities, preferring to consider men one or a few at a time, but democrats develop an ardent and lazy passion for them because they begin from the apparent fact that everyone near them is almost the same as they are—those like oneself, the *semblables*. Out of democratic equality comes the habit of thinking in terms of hasty generalization and in fear of being profound. This democratic failing prompts Tocqueville to a new discussion of religion. In volume 1 he had considered religion's utility to democracy and shown how it "teaches Americans the art of being free." In volume 2 he turns to the truth of religion.

Religion helps Americans to think by delivering them from doubt. While Descartes's philosophy imposes the requirement of doubt, especially of religion, religion in Tocqueville's eyes rescues a democratic people from the enervation and paralysis produced by doubt. Men need "very fixed ideas for themselves about God, their souls, their general duties toward their Creator and those like them," for without these they would be at the mercy of chance, subject to disorder and impotence. Religion imposes a "salutary yoke on the intellect," and if it does not save men in the next world, it is useful to their happiness and greatness in this world. It provides answers to the greatest problems, without which men, lacking the ability to think on their own, will be reduced to the cowardice of not thinking at all.

Descartes, or any philosopher, might say that doubt shows greater awareness and freedom than belief. To read Plato, one would find a less flattering view of Tocqueville's "salutary yoke" in the picture of the cave in which Socrates says most men are imprisoned. But Tocqueville says to the contrary that, for most men, doubt leads to a surrender to chance, because doubt questions whether anything happens regularly or predictably. If men believe that chance rules human events, they will let things happen as they will and not attempt mindful, free action. Religion reassures us that chance does not rule and confirms that human intentions can succeed, human actions make sense.

One could object that religion in its intellectual aspect is still judged for its utility; but now, one could answer, it is judged for the utility of the mind in directing action. Religion is good for democracy because it inspires instincts contrary to the love of material enjoyments and because, in doing so, it teaches one's duties to others. In both regards, religion is necessary to freedom. Tocqueville says he has been brought to think that "if [man] has no faith, he must serve and if he is free, he must believe." When one thinks of the hostility of the old liberalism to faith, here indeed is a "new kind of liberal." He presents religion as the public face of philosophy, rather its friend than its enemy, protecting philosophy from causing inadvertent harm—which it would do if let alone.

Pantheism is a religion-philosophy, a "philosophic system" that, as in Spinoza's system, encloses God and the universe, creator and creation, in a single whole. This means that God had to create as He did, that God is as much an effect of His creation as the cause of it. This means, too, that men are not capable of being directed by their minds, nor of being a first cause like the Puritans and are no more free than nonhuman nature. Pantheism is not only an expression of the democratic mind, as a general idea leveling all distinctions in nature and denying that there is any special status within nature for human beings. It is also an attack on the democratic mind or any notion of mind because it denies the human capacity to rise above the rest of nature by reflecting or acting on it. Pantheism is the logical culmination of scientific objectivity—giving no preference to human beings—and also, strangely enough, of democratic equality—the whole universe is democratic.

Yet immediately after his brief but important discussion of pantheism, Tocqueville brings up the idea of progress, which he calls "indefinite perfectibility." What is its relation to pantheism? Progress is the main positive belief of the democratic mind, despite its posture of doubt and its tendency toward blind fatality. Progress would seem to be mindful improvement of the status quo into something better; it would seem to be the main instance of "intellectual movement" such as he is considering. Now, progress is a human capability, distinguishing man from other animals and the rest of creation. Creation is therefore not a "single whole" as pantheism asserts, but a complex whole containing a being capable of change and creating anew—which is progress—distinct from the rest. The idea of progress is inconsistent with pantheism, and yet both are expressions of the democratic mind. Pantheism wants to generalize across all differences and distinctions, but the idea of progress insists on an exception being made of democratic men in order to show respect for the very democratic mind that is fashioning the generalization to make pantheism. Democrats say in effect that everything is essentially equal, except for the democrats who assert this point.

The inconsistency can be found within the idea of progress. Equality, Tocqueville says, *suggests* to Americans the idea of the *indefinite* perfectibility of man. Equality suggests but does not compel democrats to believe in progress, because compulsion would detract from the dignity of human invention, of conceiving and promoting a better way to be or do. And why is democratic progress indefinite? Progress can be found in aristocracy, but there it is definite; it is improvement toward perfection, or progress "within certain impassable limits." Progress cannot go beyond perfection, nor, given imperfect humans, can it do more than approach perfection.

Democracies pursue not perfection, but something different: "the image of an ideal and always fugitive perfection," an "immense greatness" always receding from view that can only be glimpsed confusedly. They do not know what perfection is, but they do not deny it either. They are unphilosophic because they deny any logic or truth outside themselves, yet at the same time they follow a "philosophic theory" of indefinite perfectibility that accepts the sovereignty of mind over matter, but awards the capability to progress to each person and every century. Tocqueville tells an anecdote of an American sailor, who explains that his country's ships are not built to last because progress is so rapid that old ships soon become useless. For Americans, the perfect ship does not exist, but somehow, without knowing what is perfect, we know vaguely, indefinitely, that new is better.

Thus the democratic mind has a theory of progress, but it is one that slights the pure theory of perfection and prefers application of theory to practice. "Equality develops the desire in each man to judge everything by himself; it gives him in all things a taste for the tangible and real and a contempt for traditions and forms." In the permanent bustle of democracy men have no leisure for the quiet meditation required for the "most theoretical principles," and they lack opinions expressing "the dignity, power, and greatness of man," that are valued in aristocracy and dispose the mind to love the truth. Tocqueville warns that progress depends on discoveries of pure theory that are less likely, though not impossible, in societies devoted to progress. Progress comes from those with a "disinterested love of truth" rather than from love of progress. Science, it appears, is not so much scientific method—the method of Americans—as love of truth. In their intellectual movement Americans do not know where they are going and have little esteem for the "contemplation of first causes" necessary for pure science. "In our day one must detain the human mind in theory," for the democratic mind prefers practice and does not to care to think profoundly on its own. In this part of *Democracy in America* Tocqueville reveals an appreciation of theory not so evident elsewhere in his book, but never absent. For the most part he describes, and then praises or blames, but here, as instructor of democracy, he presumes to give advice.

Tocqueville observes next that in cultivating the arts, Americans, though not blind to beauty, prefer the useful to the beautiful and want the beautiful to be useful. But then he makes a less obvious point by remarking on the spirit of American manufacturing. As opposed to aristocratic centuries, where the aim of the productive arts is to make the best possible product, Americans make scarcely any but mediocre ones, though everyone has one. Practicing a prudent and conscious mediocrity, their byword is "good enough," and they have discovered that you can get rich by selling cheaply to all. Still, one might wonder, how will Americans perfect their products if they do not see that to do something is to do it well? Even a mediocre product needs the model of the best if it is to improve. Tocqueville praises the painting of Raphael, a Renaissance painter he seems to consider aristocratic, for making us "glimpse divinity in his works." Divinity such as this stands above human perfection but inspires the human perfection necessary for democratic progress, yet it is not likely to be found in democratic times.

At this point Tocqueville raises the question of where greatness can be found in democracy. In democracy, individuals are weak, but the state or nation is great. Private individuals may live in small dwellings, but in their public monuments they imagine and display their desire for greatness. Americans have built for themselves an immense, artificial city (Washington, D.C.), still in Tocqueville's day scarcely more populated than a French town, for democracy typically produces many small monuments and a very few great ones, with nothing in between. Greatness in democracy is a work of expansive imagination, and his following chapters discuss democratic speech in its various forms, focusing on its characteristic exaggeration and vanity. These are the modes in which the democratic intellect expresses itself.

In literature, democratic writers despise the formal qualities of style that are prized in aristocracies. They are less artful, more bold and vehement; less erudite and profound, more imaginative and forceful; they seek to astonish rather than please, and to carry away passions rather than charm taste. One sees few great writers and thousands of vendors of ideas. The writers of antiquity, with their care for details and appeal to connoisseurs, are not much studied in democracy, where education is more scientific, commercial, and industrial than literary—though, Tocqueville adds, they are a "salutary diet" for democrats who want to excel in letters. The languages of democratic peoples reflect their desire for motion and innovation, their distaste for anything conventional and arbitrary, and their love of abstraction. Democratic poetry has an instinctive distaste for anything old and for depicting anything ideal. Instead, it opens to the future and seeks objects that are vast, such as the fate of all humanity. Democratic oratory is often bombastic, and democratic theater "becomes more striking, more vulgar, and more true"—always in comparison with aristocracy.

Yet the juxtaposition of two chapters at the end of the chapters on speech reveals the plaintive vanity at the center of the democratic intellect: how important is man when all men are equal? To answer the question, Tocqueville makes a particularly dramatic contrast between democracy and aristocracy. Historians in aristocratic centuries, he says, make all events depend on the particular wills and humors of certain men, but in democratic centuries they habitually attribute almost no influence to individuals in history and give great general causes for particular facts. It is true, he admits, that general causes explain more in democratic times, when individuals are indeed less effectual, but such explanations are dangerous because they subject individuals to an inflexible providence or a blind fatality. They imply that as man is not master of himself, he is not the master of events, thus not free. Democratic historians seem determined to show that progress is not a goal achieved consciously, voluntarily, by human beings: "Historians of antiquity instruct on how to command, those of our day teach hardly anything other than how to obey."

Yet the historians appear great themselves, seeming to dispose of the great causes they describe and complacently looking down on the rest of humanity unaware of the forces driving them forward. The following chapter on parliamentary eloquence in the United States looks to be unconnected to history but actually develops the same thought. In aristocratic parliaments the members, being aristocrats, have nothing to prove and are content to remain silent if they have nothing to say. In America, on the contrary, the representative is a nobody and is constantly stung by the necessity to acquire and display his importance as well as that of his electors, holding forth with frequent pompous and incompetent orations. The spirit of the democratic representative, who says that *he* is important, contradicts the spirit of the democratic historians, who presume that *man* is insignificant. Democratic man, it appears, has a desire to be honored, a desire unknown to himself to live in an aristocracy, where he would be honored as someone important. His generalizing mind, busy at justifying democracy, is at odds with his own individual mind justifying himself.

Democratic individualism

Moving from ideas to "sentiments," Tocqueville examines the feelings that characterize the democratic heart. The main one is a sense of weakness that he describes as "individualism." This is a word we now hear every day and in several senses, usually in a good sense, as in "rugged individualism." Tocqueville was not the first to use the word, but he was the first to make a point of it. He defines it in contrast to egoism or selfishness, a passionate self-love that is universally a moral vice. Individualism is democratic sentiment, reflective and peaceable, that disposes each citizen to isolate himself from the mass of his fellow citizens and to withdraw into his family, his friends, and himself. It is accompanied by the passion for equality, always stronger in a democracy than the taste for liberty, but it is itself more an erroneous judgment than a passion or a vice. That judgment, proceeding from the democratic social state, is the same one taught by the pantheists and the democratic historians: that the individual is impotent, that he is subject to vast, impersonal forces, and that public virtues are futile. Unlike aristocracy, where hierarchy binds men to one another and to the past, democracy puts them on a level so that, although they extend their good will abstractly and weakly to all humanity, they in fact take interest only in those nearest to them.

Not having endured a democratic revolution, Americans have less individualism than democratic peoples in Europe; in Tocqueville's phrase, they had the great advantage "to be born equal instead of becoming so." Since they are aware of their individualism, they "combat" it with free associations and with the strange moral doctrine of self-interest well understood, both of which he discussed in volume 1. Associations draw men from the private ease of individualism into public activity, engaging their self-interest and their ambition while promoting the common good.

The doctrine Tocqueville describes is again "self-interest well understood." It comes from American moralists prescribing for Americans, he says, and it is "of all philosophic theories the most appropriate to the needs of men in our time." It accommodates human weaknesses by turning personal interest against itself: "to

68

direct the passions, it makes use of the spur that excites them."
Yet despite the doctrine's ingenuity, he lets his doubts be seen
in the contrast of democracy to aristocracy. Under aristocracy,
men spoke of the beauties of virtue and secretly studied its
usefulness, but now under democracy, the relation is reversed,
and American moralists fear speaking of the beauties of virtue.
Virtue that is beautiful might call for sacrifice, and democratic
moralists, not daring to recommend that, search for an instance
in which virtue is in one's self-interest and expand it into a general
doctrine. Tocqueville names no American moralist, citing only
Montaigne, but the most obvious American teacher of self-
interest well understood would be Benjamin Franklin. Franklin's
Autobiography shows how to make one's way up in the world
while seeking only to help others and concealing all ambition.

Tocqueville in his analysis brings to the fore a subtle point that
Franklin also makes, but not so conspicuously. He shows that in
America it is not so much that self-interest needs to conceal itself
as virtue—which is ordinary hypocrisy practiced in all human
societies—but that in America, virtue needs to conceal itself as
self-interest. To claim virtue in a democracy is to expose oneself as
better than one's "similars" and thus to make oneself a target for
envy. Tocqueville says that Americans "would rather do honor to
their philosophy than to themselves," that is, would rather admit
than deny they are self-interested. "Do honor to their philosophy"
means do honor to the truth. But where does truth come from?
Not from oneself. The doctrine of self-interest does not come
from self-interest but from a disinterested pursuit of truth. So
Americans contradict themselves; they *are* honoring themselves
as acting on principle rather than interest despite their disclaimer.
And Tocqueville, in praising Americans for their practice of
political liberty, does the reverse of what he says Americans do: he
honors Americans rather than their philosophy.

Self-interest well understood is not only contradictory but
also too abstract. It implies that there is a universal human

"self" that always acts or reacts in the same way. Tocqueville maintains, however, that this supposedly universal self is actually the democratic soul. In the series of chapters following the one on self-interest well understood, he again considers the taste for material well-being characteristic of democratic soul. He concludes that democracy produces a decent, moderate materialism that does not corrupt souls so much as it softens them. Americans are dissatisfied and "restive" (*inquiets*—a frequent term in Tocqueville) in the midst of their prosperity. Their belief in the doctrine of "self-interest" is not justified by human nature but determined by the democracy in which they live, and it is not in fact "well understood" by them.

In view of the typical restiveness of Americans, it is important that they have something long-term to work for—Tocqueville's next topic. It is the task of religion to free democrats, as much as possible, from the scramble for immediate satisfactions and to give them the habit of acting for a goal in the future. And when democracy is irreligious, because of its love of material well-being, this is also the task of "philosophers and those who govern." It is necessary to "banish chance as much as possible from the political world," not by using science to predict what will happen regardless of our desires, but to give the impression that honest effort will be rewarded. The belief that chance rules the world keeps a people passive and inert, whether because it makes virtuous sacrifice too risky if you think you are unlucky, or because it makes success seem too easy if you think you are lucky. Although chance cannot and should not be altogether banished from human life, since this would banish freedom as well, it should be reduced to the point where humans can reasonably believe they are sovereign over their affairs and in charge of their lives. Tocqueville sets this single guiding function for religion, philosophy, and politics alike. Governments must teach citizens that "great successes are found at the end of long-lasting desires." Thinking about their future in this world will bring them back, without being conscious of it, to faith in the next world. Virtue of the American kind, however disguised as self-interest, as long as it is lasting, can be shown not to be a dream or a gift of chance, but even grounded in the natural order of things. With merited "great successes," the American belief in endless perfectibility would be rescued from its restless anxiety and would receive some validation in reasonable confidence.

Never one to promise too much, however, Tocqueville fears that the American future may hold a new aristocracy created by industry. Much like Karl Marx, he anticipates that the democratic worker will be reduced to obedience and dependency as increasing division of labor narrows his vision and capacity, so that all planning and thinking is reserved for the industrial master. Such an aristocracy would be harsh, because it treats workers as things, but not dangerous, because it would not be organized in a ruling class. It is in the nature of democracy—Tocqueville does not speak of capitalism—to inspire instability and the love of chance. That is why democracies turn to commerce, which they do not merely for gain but for fun. Industrial crises are in the democratic temperament, hence impossible to foresee and endemic in democracy. The American dream of virtue rewarded is endangered by the complexity of commerce and subject to sudden surprise.

Two lasting democratic sentiments are revealed in Tocqueville's discussion and shown to be fundamentally irrational: the taste for material well-being and the passion for equality. The first flits endlessly, the second makes unceasing demands, and neither is capable of being satisfied. Both tend to weaken democratic individuals, the first by enervating souls and the second by depriving all authority and obedience of legitimacy. Yet by practicing political freedom and acting for the public good together with their interest, Americans show that they are serious about a whole of which they are parts and are not merely wholes by themselves. They refute "individualism" in their deeds without being aware of their virtue, or without realizing they would do better to acknowledge and claim their virtue. In advising them contrary to their moralists, Tocqueville would help them to understand their self-interest well.

Mores of equality

Tocqueville proceeds from ideas to sentiments to mores, each inspiring the next—mores being the behavior suggested by thought and prompted by feeling. In this part of his wonderful book he considers how democracy deals with stubborn inequalities that nature (the word occurs frequently) seems to set against it. What of the relation between master and servant under democracy? The apparent superiority of men to women? The desire for honor that craves distinction over others? In each case democracy does its best to equalize the inequalities, putting its best face on them, making them less harsh, less imperious, and less odious. It does not succeed in doing away with inequality but gives it a stamp reminding all of the fundamental truth of human equality underlying the compromise with inequality. At the same time democracy, even as it equalizes, supplies its own justification for these inequalities, and thus seems to admit that equality can go only so far and that human inequality is also a fundamental truth.

Tocqueville begins with his usual contrast, declaring that as social conditions become more equal, mores become milder and gentler than under aristocracy. He illustrates the point with one of the most striking passages in his book, quoting from the correspondence of Madame de Sévigné, an aristocrat of the seventeenth century, with her daughter. She gaily relates, amid gossip of the day, an incident of a taxpayers' revolt crushed by the torturing and hanging of those chiefly responsible and by expulsion of the rest, "all those miserable people," from their homes. His comment: "Madame de Sévigné did not clearly conceive what it was to suffer when one was not a gentleman." This passage should be read by anyone who believes that

Tocqueville was too favorable to aristocracy. Democratic compassion takes the edge off democratic self-interest and is surely part of self-interest well understood. But democrats too have their blindness to suffering, as in their behavior to slaves and to enemies in war, when they do not see themselves in those suffering, when they do not recognize others to be "similar."

Master and servant under aristocracy are permanently unequal, but in democracy they are only temporarily so because they are unequal only by contract, not by class or family. The aristocratic servant therefore takes on the personality of his master, his dignity derivative from his master's, his mores as haughty or sometimes more so. The democratic servant has no such penchant for proud servility; his dignity lies in the equality he shares with his master outside the limits of the contract, where master and servant are "two citizens, two men." But which—equal as citizens or as men?

Tocqueville says that the two are brought near to each other despite their apparent distance by public opinion, which "creates a sort of imaginary equality between them." Democracy is not quite in accord with nature, it seems; the natural equality that democrats allege needs a push from public opinion, which asserts that men are equal regardless of their station. Master and servant are two citizens who want to be no more than two men, the equality of nature not quite sufficient by itself, but in need of the convention of citizenship aiming at the equality of nature. Democratic equality is possible because democratic public opinion says it is. We see a political truth emerging from the discussion of a relationship in civil society: the social contract of official liberal theory, creating a distinction between those who command and those who obey, is not made by the consent of equal individuals in a state of nature but by citizens who are asserted by public opinion to be equal human beings. In Tocqueville's version, the contract does not create society but begins from it, and it does not assume the equality of human nature but attempts to preserve and in some measure to establish it.

The same political version of the social contract, the same correction of its official liberal version, can be pursued in Tocqueville's remarkable discussion of American women. Liberal theory before Tocqueville spoke of the "rights of man," meaning of human beings abstracted from sex. In our day this theory has come under attack for being too abstract, for overlooking the traditional, supposedly natural, inequality of women to men. Pre-Tocqueville liberals had little to say about that inequality, often seeming to take it for granted. Tocqueville corrects this neglect with five chapters on American women, praising them to the skies for their virtue and good works. There is no free society without mores, he says, and women make mores. Men pass laws, but mores are more important than laws. In his eyes there is "great political interest" in everything to do with American women.

The trouble is that Tocqueville praises American women for keeping out of politics and forsaking careers—anathema to most of them today. But one should not dismiss his reasoning merely because its conclusion is distasteful. There is more to be learned about Tocqueville's new liberalism from his discussion of women.

The influence of democracy on the family is to destroy paternal authority in the aristocratic sense, which is true "patriarchy" well beyond today's meaning of the term. Democracy equalizes father and child, overthrowing natural differences of age and sex, yet resulting in the tightening of natural bonds within the family even as peremptory authority disappears. Young girls, freed of their father's protective control, learn to manage on their own, controlling their own passions and developing their own judgment, soon losing their naiveté (of which they have less than a philosopher) and acquiring a "precocious knowledge of all things." They have, Tocqueville says memorably, "pure mores rather than a chaste mind." They pick up an education in mores by watching the world—the world of men, thus acquiring a manly education to replace the paternal authority they lack. Manliness is not solely a male quality, according to Tocqueville.

Yet when women marry they enter upon matrimony, whose "bonds," both moral and domestic, Tocqueville gives particular emphasis. In America, he says, women have a completely different destiny from that of men, for which they must abandon the light and free spirit of a girl and find happiness in the home with its duties and constraints. American women suffer the bonds of matrimony bravely, however, because they have chosen willingly to accept them. Tocqueville makes a point of their choice—the very word used today to describe a quite different life for women, in which they are not merely permitted, but invited and encouraged, to leave the home for a career or a job. For him, choice is not an escape from woman's separate destiny but a choice of with whom to live as a wife; though a woman will in most cases marry, she has the choice of a husband and does not have to accept the one chosen for her by her father. Here, in describing a choice we take for granted, Tocqueville lets us know that a free choice needs to be made wisely. Since divorce was rare in that day, a woman was not free to make a mistake and correct it; she had to be careful and responsible. A man would not so much choose a wife as be attracted to a woman, but the marriage was made by the woman's choice: a difference in the ways in which men and women approach marriage perhaps still noticeable today.

To make her choice and to live in her marriage a woman has the free exercise of her reason as well as the aid of religion, and in regard to women as everywhere in Tocqueville's book, reason and religion cooperate. Although he said in volume 1 that religion reigns as sovereign in a woman's soul, he now shows that this sovereignty is shared with reason. Partly due to the influence of Protestantism in America, partly also due to women's worldly education, religion there does not keep women in a state of credulous dependence on fathers, husbands, and clergy. American women are independent despite living under the "yoke" of marriage, and they practice what Tocqueville calls "virtue" and are today called "family values" by choice and reason rather than by submission to religious authority.

7. A page from Tocqueville's original manuscript of *Democracy in America*. Here Tocqueville discusses American women, in a chapter from the second volume called "How the Girl Is Found Beneath the Features of the Wife."

In America women think that a marriage needs a head, and that "the most natural head of the conjugal association is the man." The "most virtuous women" there glory in the "voluntary abandonment of their wills" (they *say* this) and are therefore much esteemed, while in Europe, where women are more in authority (even holding a "despotic empire"), they are regarded as weak creatures who must seduce men to get what they want. The "great inequality of man and woman" has until our time seemed to have "its eternal foundations in nature," a change Tocqueville does not challenge. He endorses it in the form it takes in America—or in the form he says he finds in America—with ringing words: "If one asked me to what do I think one must principally attribute the singular prosperity and growing force of this people, I would answer that it is to the superiority of its women." Quite a tribute! He does not say whether American women are superior to other women or to American men; maybe it's both.

American women today, insofar as they are eager for careers and anxious for status, are no doubt willing to forego Tocqueville's praise of their virtue in a sense now almost obsolete. But one should not overlook its philosophic content. Democracy stands for the sovereignty of the people, which we have seen requires the sovereignty of human beings. Humans cannot escape necessity or fate, however, and human sovereignty requires that human choice be shown to be compatible with external powers that may seem to imprison or enslave humans. Tocqueville, in his beautiful, perhaps exaggerated picture, presented as fact but more *ought* than *is*, assigns to American women the task of choosing to accept necessity with dignity. He opposes the social contract of liberal theory, which overlooks the human necessity of living together and tries to make it appear to be a choice, as if one could choose everything. In its place he offers the marriage contract and shows how it might work through the example and speech of American women.

Human greatness and democratic despotism

At the end of his master work on democracy, Tocqueville discloses the political evil toward which democracy naturally tends, the culmination of his fear, repeatedly expressed, that democratic equality will overwhelm democratic freedom. Here, he calls

this evil "mild despotism"; elsewhere he calls it democratic or
administrative despotism. It is an attractive, not a menacing,
evil, soft, passive, and even apparently beneficent, replacing the
tyranny of the majority as his main fear (in volume 1), which in
the form of slavery is harsh and oppressive. We have seen the
germ of mild despotism in his description in volume 1 of the vague
power of public opinion, but in volume 2 we see it embodied in
the centralized democratic state.

Mild despotism is not inevitable, and it is not unopposed in
democracy. There is a counterforce to it in human nature, and
Tocqueville begins the last part of the book with an argument that
equality *naturally* gives men a taste for free institutions rather
than despotism. Equality, he says, makes them independent
of one another, hence suspicious of authority and disposed to
follow nobody's will but their own. Equality inspires a certain
unruliness *(indocilité)*, a willful "don't tread on me" that recalls
the spirited part of the soul in Plato *(thumos)* and that is favorable
to democratic insistence on liberty. Unruliness might seem
contrary to the American penchant for associations, and it can
be, but its negative refusal to cooperate can be made responsible
when people see usefulness and dignity in accomplishing some
task. One might say today that Americans are generally hostile to
authority, in that way difficult to govern, yet also have an opposed
spirit of "can do" in particular situations.

Despite the intractability in human nature that makes any
government difficult, democracy naturally tends in the
opposite direction toward making government easier and more
agreeable. Tocqueville's anxiety arising from loss of the taste for
free institutions is the theme of the last part of *Democracy in
America*. The democrat, we know, readily becomes a victim of
individualism, the enervating sentiment of weakness that turns
citizens into isolated individuals concerned only with their private
lives. When they do this, the state is left as the only visible and
permanent representative of the community, and individuals

leave their associations as they develop a natural inclination to let the state take care of all common affairs. As equals they have an instinct toward pride and independence, but as individuals they suffer a sense of weakness and isolation that results from independence. Hence they turn away from local activity in politics and society and deliver their apathetic obedience to the "immense being" of the state (a term Tocqueville had used earlier for the god of pantheism).

While every democratic people tends toward dependence on the state, the state for its part loves equality and extends it as much as it can. The modern state had its origin in the monarchies of Europe that followed a policy of allying with the people against the aristocracy, gradually removing them from the government of barons and nobles to the central administration of the state. When monarchy was replaced by democracy during the French Revolution, the state remained the same and continued to appropriate all administration to itself, as its new hostility to associations replaced monarchical jealousy of the aristocracy. Thus the centralized state loves the equality that democratic citizens love and hates what they hate; the two mutually reinforce each other. The state constantly reinforces power; the people continuously lose it.

The sort of despotism democratic nations have to fear, then, is mild. Far from frustrating their desires, it satisfies the worst of them. The worst desire in democracy is abandonment of the pride that sustains one's independence and loss of freedom, thus degrading men without tormenting them, without arousing their opposition or even giving them notice of what they have lost. They become a "crowd of like and equal men...procuring the small and vulgar pleasures with which they fill their souls." Each is "withdrawn and apart," existing "only in himself and for himself alone." Above them "an immense tutelary power is elevated," which takes charge of them in the manner of a schoolmaster or guardian, sparing them, Tocqueville says with splendid sarcasm, "the trouble of thinking and the pain of living." Anticipating Nietzsche, he calls them a "herd of timid and industrious animals of which the government is the shepherd."

In this condition a democratic people feels both the need to be free and the need to be led, and it consoles itself for being led with the thought that they have chosen their leaders. When participating in elections they leave their dependency for a moment, only to return to it afterwards. "That does not suffice for me," Tocqueville says proudly in his own name.

Certain accidental facts, Tocqueville admits, can increase or decrease the drive toward centralization of government—the democratic revolution that did not occur in America, for example. Because America was not obliged to mount a democratic revolution against an aristocracy—having been born equal without having to become so—it was freer to borrow from aristocracy to support its liberty. Near the end of his book Tocqueville mentions three features of equality that democratic peoples need to be watchful of. The first is the utility of forms already discussed, which democracies do not readily understand and for which they feel disdain. A second democratic instinct, also very natural and said to be very dangerous, is to scorn individual rights and to sacrifice them to the interests and power of society. Speaking as a liberal, Tocqueville says that the "true friends of liberty and human greatness" must always be on guard to ensure that individual rights are not lightly sacrificed to the general designs of society. To do so is actually harmful to society because it questions the basis of society as the supporter of rights.

Connected to these two fears, Tocqueville adds his concern for revolutions in democratic societies, a concern perhaps more acute for Europe than America. Since democracies love change, revolution can become a habit and even regularized in government policy. He does not deny that revolution is sometimes honest and legitimate, but he thinks it a particularly dangerous remedy in democratic times. He had spoken earlier of why great revolutions will become rare, such as a revolution against democracy, saying that he feared stagnation more than violent commotion from the middle class that tends to prevail in democracies. But stagnation in democracy is not incompatible with a universal, low-level agitation of mediocre ambition and competition for material enjoyments.

What is the remedy for democratic individualism, democratic mediocrity, and democratic apathy? The answer leaps out of the phrase quoted above describing Tocqueville's particular addressees: "the true friends of liberty and of human greatness." It is the cooperation of liberty and human greatness. At first one will think of mixing the liberty of democracy with the greatness of aristocracy in a mixed regime of the classical sort. But as always in *Democracy in America*, and especially at the end, Tocqueville insists that democracy is here to stay, that there is no possibility of "reconstructing an aristocratic society," that one must show oneself to be a friend of equality and adopt unmixed democracy as one's "first principle and creed." So he does not appeal here to great men, "the greatness of a few," as inspiration for democracy. He does not recall the American founders he had praised, the Federalists whom he called an aristocratic party. Instead he says that though one cannot found an aristocracy anew, he thinks "that when plain citizens associate, they can constitute very opulent, very influential, very strong beings—in a word, aristocratic persons."

Free association of plain citizens creates the aristocracy of democracy. They are its nobles; they exercise their freedom and in so doing stand up for it, defend it, and display it. By associating they make sacrifices and take the risks in public ambition not incurred by those who combine in merely commercial organizations. Though plain citizens do have something to gain from politics, the reward they receive is just as much a feeling of pride as it is profit in money. Americans are surely bourgeois, restless and avid for gain as Tocqueville describes them, but when they get together in free associations they have something of nobility in their souls. Here is the answer of democracy, impressive if not fully adequate, to the charges against it of apathy and mediocrity.

Thus the danger that the true friends of freedom and human greatness must be ready to prevent is that "the social power" will lightly sacrifice individual rights to the execution of a social purpose. "No citizen is so obscure that it is not very dangerous to allow him to be oppressed." Yet the main protections for the obscure citizen cited here by Tocqueville are the freedom of the press and the judicial power. He now says, exceeding the measured praise he expressed earlier in his book, that a free press is "infinitely more precious in democratic nations than in all others." A free press enables individuals to communicate with fellow citizens, thus to rise from obscurity. The judiciary has the task of listening to obscure citizens when they feel oppressed. Here one sees an unidentified, unnamed aristocracy at work in democracy to support individual rights, perhaps against the more strictly democratic parts of the government, the legislature and the executive branch, who represent "the social power."

The "first object of the legislator" in the democratic age is to fix limits for social power that are "extended, but visible and immoveable." The "legislator" would seem to be someone who is above the legislature, perhaps a political scientist such as Tocqueville himself. For such a figure fixing limits to the social power includes the making of a constitution but also, it appears, the defense of democracy against ideas that promote the social power against the individual. For all his earlier insistence on the social state as the first cause of democracy, he now identifies "two contrary but equally fatal ideas" that may arise from the democratic social state but that endanger it. The first is that democracy is nothing but its anarchical tendencies; those who hold it are afraid of their free will, "afraid of themselves." The

Tocqueville

82

second is that democracy necessarily leads to servitude, and its proponents despair of remaining free and secretly adore the despotism they believe to be inevitable.

In this bare description of the two ideas, Tocqueville names no names and gives little material from which readers might guess them. As usual, he looks more at their consequences than their content. Nonetheless, he ends his great book by denouncing two "false and cowardly doctrines" that imperil the democracy he has found in America. He declares, more in the style of Aristotle than of his own predecessors in liberalism, that Providence has not created the human race "either entirely independent or perfectly slave."

Chapter 5
Rational administration

Tocqueville's second great work, *The Old Regime and the Revolution*, was published in 1856. In it he considers the Old Regime of the French monarchy, but he does not reach the Revolution, and the book remained unfinished when he died in 1859. He studies the Old Regime with a view to the French Revolution—as it prepared the Revolution. The Old Regime gradually brought about its own ruin over twenty generations with the institution of rational administration, which we might call government by meritocracy. Rational administration in Tocqueville's conception is the counterpart to democracy, and we have seen it as centralized administration in *Democracy in America*.

In this later work Tocqueville elaborates the meaning and techniques of big government. He reveals that it is not merely a fearful image of the future, conjured up by enemies of democracy, but an actual historical fact in France. The French monarchy did not intend to establish a democracy, but it did the work of democracy nonetheless. By gradually abolishing the feudal order in which the nobles ruled in their local domains, the French kings and their great ministers Cardinals Richelieu and Mazarin first leveled all citizens, then reordered them in a new, nonfeudal hierarchy of the centralized modern state under which the French—and to a varying extent all democratic peoples—live today.

The democratic revolution in France of 1789 was a vast unintended consequence of the policy of the French kings and the inaction of the French nobility, which together modernized France without meaning to. Democracy in France was monarchy come to perdition in sudden and violent revolution through the logic of its own fundamental strategy of allying with the people against the nobles. Its political strategy came to be conjoined with the plans of "men of letters" for reform through rational administration. These abstract reformers were fundamentally apolitical, but they favored monarchy as the instrument of reform and dismissed democracy as vulgar, ignorant, and opposed to reform. Democracy, then, was the consequence of two allied powers, monarchy and reformers, who were opposed to democracy and united only by their common hostility to aristocracy. The great advance of human reason against the feudal regime of privilege and prejudice—interpreted by the philosopher Hegel as man's final assertion of his own sovereign thought—came about as an accident, or a consequence, unforeseen by all parties. This is the brilliant and startling argument of Tocqueville's *Old Regime*.

Tocqueville first mentioned the idea for his book late in 1850 in a letter to his friend Louis Kergorlay, speaking of a study of the "long drama of the French Revolution." Two years later he would refer to his 1842 speech at the French Academy attacking the influence of Napoleon as "the most perfected despotism" in world history and also denouncing the abstract ideas behind the Revolution. Together, these two points suggested the outcome and the origin of the Revolution into which he was about to inquire. Even earlier, in 1836, while enjoying the success of the first volume of *Democracy in America*, he had written an essay on France before and since 1789 that had been commissioned by John Stuart Mill and published in Mill's *London and Westminster Review*. From his first conception of the book in 1850, he moved his focus backward in time from Napoleon to the Directory (after the Revolution) to the Old Regime, settling on the latter in August 1853.

Tocqueville set to work in January 1852, reading memoirs and making notes. In June 1853, he saw the need to consult the archives of the Old Regime and spent a year in the city of Tours poring over the records of the key officials in its administration, the Intendants. The work of reading books and pamphlets and of mining in dusty archives is almost entirely covered over by the elegant polish and striking phrases of his book. Robert Gannett, in his superb study of the book, *Tocqueville Unveiled*, uncovers the evidence behind it and remarks on the "secretive mode" of its author. His many notes and quotations are mainly illustrative and the sources are usually not cited. At the same time, Tocqueville frequently reminds his readers of the work he has done, one could almost say boasts of it, as if challenging them to make their own search unguided.

Tocqueville begins by calling his work a "study." But what kind of study? It is more directly historical than *Democracy in America*, which begins from a "providential fact," the mounting trend toward ever more democracy, and argues from the premise that the image of democracy is to be found in America. At the end of that book he raises the specter of mild despotism, but he shows it from the standpoint of the people, explaining why they welcome the stifling embrace of big government, and he describes the remedies for it practiced by Americans. He then declares that he responsibly accepts democracy, despite its faults, asserting that there is no alternative in a democratic age and, besides, that it shows greater justice than aristocracy. *The Old Regime* looks at the same despotism, now referred to as "democratic despotism," from the standpoint of the king and the nobles. They brought about a democracy neither party desired, inflicted on them with horrifying violence by a revolution no one anticipated. This book emphatically deplores the loss of aristocracy, which resulted in a "nation" composed of an incoherent mass of angry or frightened citizens. It details the strategic avarice of kings and the idle abnegation of nobles, while praising only the aspects of French society these two parties neglected to touch with their corrupt meddling and complacency.

Both works are political in the sense of offering advice to France, and to all, but in *The Old Regime* the author lets go his indignation and shows little of the calm impartiality that distinguishes *Democracy in America*. He is angry not so much at the Revolution as at the old monarchy it replaced, and not so much at the old monarchy as at the unfolding of both monarchy and revolution in the despotism of Napoleon. One could cap the point by observing that the upshot of the rule of Napoleon was the bourgeois mediocrity of the empire of his nephew Louis Napoleon.

The Old Regime has been aptly called "political history" because it combines political judgment and history while avoiding polemics and stultifying scientific objectivity. Yet these are differences of form, not substance. *The Old Regime* should be seen as the application to France of the same thoroughgoing concern for the requirements of political liberty that can be found in *Democracy in America*. Whereas in that book he starts from the providential trend toward democracy, which may or may not be favorable to liberty, in the foreword of this one he launches himself, he avows, in passion for the defense of liberty and in support of those higher, energetic passions that liberty looses in its defense. In the rest of the book his passion for liberty is justified by his inquiry, as it turns out that politics and liberty are inseparable, that the loss of liberty in France followed inevitably from the loss of political liberty under the monarchy. Two points of political science left undeveloped in *Democracy in America* are set forth in *The Old Regime*: the aristocratic roots of political liberty, and the danger to it arising from rational administration. But it is best to begin from the main historical thesis of *The Old Regime*.

The continuity of the Revolution

The French Revolutionaries thought of themselves as having made a complete break with the past. They intended to cut the destiny of their country in two parts unrecognizable to one another, before and after 1789, and believed they had succeeded. Opposing them, the counterrevolutionaries believed the same thing. Edmund Burke, the great British statesman and philosopher whom Tocqueville chooses as his foil throughout *The Old Regime*, declared that the French Revolution was "the first, complete revolution" in history. It was a revolution in sentiments, manners, and moral opinions that reached "even to the constitution of the human mind." Tocqueville takes up against this point of agreement on both sides and argues that the Revolution came from the society it was to destroy, and that it was the work of the Old Regime of the French monarchy, which bent itself to the task of deliberately, yet as a whole unconsciously, destroying itself. The Revolution did not just take place in 1789 with the fall of the Bastille; it had been under way since the day in 1439 (or 1444) when Charles VII was able to order a new tax without the consent of the nobility.

Yet Tocqueville does not deny that a great change occurred. He denies that it occurred by human intention either on the part of the revolutionaries or against the will of their opponents. For the democratic historians decried in *Democracy in America* for their denial of human intention in history are right about the coming of democracy. The title, *The Old Regime and the Revolution*, indicates the magnitude of the change, omitting to specify the *French* Revolution. (Tocqueville was worried about the title and just before publication seems to have removed, or consented to the removal of, the adjective.) He agrees that the Revolution was complete, as Burke said, and was preached to other nations as for the attention of mankind, like the American Revolution. It would not be repeated or cancelled by future revolutions and in fact was meant to bring to completion all previous revolutions, which were incomplete and which therefore invited further revolutions to restore the past. What he insists is that this great change had been under way for centuries; it was new but not recent. It should not have been a surprise. In his book he shows the actions that produced it, but whose overall meaning escaped the notice of all as they were made. After 1789 the meaning

8. Edmund Burke, British statesman and philosopher. In *The Old Regime*, Tocqueville contrasts Burke's analysis of the French Revolution with his own.

was covered over by the boasting of the revolutionaries and the denunciations of their enemies.

Those observers of the Revolution who were able to recover from their surprise most often thought that it was meant to destroy religion and to bring on anarchy or at least weaken political power. Burke, the outstanding example of this view, concentrated his fire on the atheism of its projectors, who he said were transforming mankind by removing the belief that there is a power above men, thus weakening government by denying it divine sanction. For Tocqueville, this is to mistake an accident for something fundamental. The church was perhaps the most powerful part of the Old Regime; it was in the way of reform and had to be attacked, in both institution and belief, to make possible a new order replacing the Old Regime. This new order was the fundamental object, not the destruction of the church, and it was to be stronger, not weaker than the old order. France had no intention to tear itself into pieces, and in fact it later formed an army more powerful than any it had ever had, and it fashioned a new revolutionary religion of the Supreme Being that it hoped would be more authoritative than Christianity. The French Revolution, Tocqueville says later in the book, was more like the Protestant Reformation than any other previous event, and it expected to claim for itself the support that Christianity had offered to the Old Regime, and with greater enthusiasm as well. Just as in *Democracy in America*, Tocqueville wants it to be known that there is no necessary antagonism between religion and liberty, not even between the contrived religion and false liberty of the Revolution.

Why the French Revolution was the first revolution to make this attack and to assume the character of a new religion, Tocqueville does not say directly. Apparently the ideas it acted on became more acceptable to more people, so that at a certain point the theory seemed viable. The French Revolution, as a complete revolution surpassing all previous revolutions, was not based on a truer idea than any held before but rather was suddenly seen to be viable and the Old Regime not. The Old Regime was feudalism, and feudalism after a certain development Tocqueville will describe came to be seen no longer as a stable and coherent whole capable of sustaining itself. At that point, as Americans might say today, it no longer seemed practical. In his political history Tocqueville rejects the attempt of the revolutionary thinkers to make theory precede practice. He does not attempt to judge the competing ideas supporting and attacking feudalism, but instead considers whether feudalism constituted a whole that could be the subject of an idea, of a reasonable theory. Again, as in his first book he studied the practices of Americans to discover the image of democracy, so in this one he considers the practices of the Old Regime to see whether they were coherent.

At first, feudalism was a confusion of barbarous tribes living in isolation from one another, but from that emerged a particular Germanic legislation, an original creation not due to Roman law, which formed "a body composed of parts," as closely linked as modern codes, sage laws for the use of a society half-barbaric. Tocqueville does not say how the elaborate hierarchy of privileges and duties in feudalism came about; he only says that both code and hierarchy were the same almost everywhere in Europe, having no assignable cause, as if they were a spontaneous, natural development. This, not the France of the eighteenth century, was the true Old Regime, and it was *this* that the true revolution overturned. The true revolution was the administrative centralization of the French monarchy, the fundamental institution of both the Old Regime and the French Revolution as those terms are commonly used.

What was administrative centralization? If one examines the first step taken by Charles VII, mentioned earlier, one sees the king gaining the power to tax without the consent of the nobility, in exchange for the exemption of the nobility from the tax. The nobility sells its political power and the king buys it, out of avarice,

Tocqueville says. But in addition, there is on the king's side "the instinct that carries every government to wish to lead all its affairs alone, an instinct that always remains the same through diverse agents." This motive goes beyond the accident of avarice, for it tempts any government to suck the power from any association not derived from itself. Over centuries the nobility continued to lose its power to be consulted and to govern in its own domains to the monarchy, which learned to govern through Intendants, administrative officials who were agents of the king and directed from the center by his ministers.

Intendants became the characteristic officers of the Old Regime (as it had become), chosen for merit and developing a skill in "inventing a thousand means of control." They were from the middle class because the nobility disdained a situation so inferior and subordinate, preferring to compete with one another at the court for the king's favor. The Intendants kept careful records of what they did and tried to do, studied carefully by Tocqueville in the archives at Paris. These administrators were the "aristocracy of the new society," and he calls them *fonctionnaires*, or civil servants. Like modern bureaucrats (and he has a remark in his notes disparaging that "modern jargon"), they have a taste for statistics and accounts. To show their humanity, they raise their eyes from reckoning their figures to complain about the lazy perversity of the peasants who were often little disposed to follow their advice or accept their instructions. In the eighteenth century, they even showed some of the "false sensibility" of Diderot and Rousseau, which tries to take the edge off a dry rendering of accounts, rather like the therapeutic effusions of management psychology today. He tells the story of a controller-general directing a government program of charity providing funds that the inhabitants of parishes had to match with their own contributions. When the amount was sufficient, the official wrote in the margin: *good, express satisfaction*; when it was unusually large, he wrote: *good, express satisfaction and sensibility*.

Tocqueville

92

From the anecdote we see that administrative centralization in the Old Regime was not harsh or tyrannical. As it became more detailed and more extensive, it became more regular, more knowing, and more moderate. "It oppresses less, it leads more." This is the mild despotism Tocqueville warned of in *Democracy in America*. It is benign and instructive, its power tutelary rather than malevolent. It pretended to teach peasants "the art of getting rich," distributing little writings on the art of agriculture. Tocqueville finds in this the origin of what was later called in France "tutelary administration" (*la tutelle administrative*), suggesting the care of a guardian, the teaching of a tutor. Americans today will think of the U. S. Department of Agriculture. The rub was (and perhaps still is) that the government promises more improvement than it can deliver, the people become skeptics, the supposed rationality of new methods looks ridiculous, and all the French are kept *en tutelle,* deprived of the benefits of self-government. In this situation the government often hesitated and lost its nerve, and so the Old Regime was typically run by rigid rules, with weak enforcement made even more lax by privileges and exemptions.

Paris was the center of the administrative state and, in its sovereign preponderance over the rest of France, the symbol of centralization. The city grew in size over the years despite attempts by the kings to restrain it. As public life and local freedoms in the provinces disappeared, Paris became the sole center of power, and with that the arbiter of taste. It was a growing site of industry, too, since regulation there was less confining than in the provinces. When the Revolution came, it took place in Paris, the capital city deciding for all of France—so that the dominance of that city was among the chief causes of the sudden and violent fall of the old monarchy.

These were the main qualities of administrative centralization. The overall result, which in time became the government's intent, Tocqueville maintains, was nothing less than to do away with politics and substitute administration in its place.

Beginning as a product of avarice in the kings and the nobility, then developing into the effect of an instinct common to all government, the French monarchy's administration appears finally as a momentous change, truly a revolution in political history even if not planned. This new kind of government takes the place of God's Providence; it establishes a relationship with each person as an individual, no longer as a member of a class, as under feudalism. They are rather like the entitlements of the present-day welfare state, which also are benefits that go from the government directly to individuals, bypassing all intermediate groups. This means that the individual looks only to government, as if praying to God, instead of to his family or his status in the feudal hierarchy. There are no "secondary powers" between the government and the individual that might stand up to the central authority in order to defend rights and privileges of the individual as member of a group, such as a noble or a serf who depends on a noble. There are no *associations* such as Tocqueville found in America, serving the function of nobles in an aristocracy by providing a check on authority strangely similar to that of the feudal order in the Middle Ages, by which kings were limited and tyranny prevented.

As the monarchy advanced, the French nobility declined, avaricious like the kings but more short-sighted. Originally the nobles traded their right to consent to a tax for an exemption from the tax once it was imposed. Some later taxes were imposed on all but still with indulgence for the nobility. This led to a situation in which the rich paid no taxes and lost their sense of responsibility for those they no longer helped to support. They lost much of their wealth too, because the king began to sell offices at the court to them; the nobles foolishly prized the honors of courtly life over the pleasures and duties of governing their dependents. Needing more money, the nobles then sold their land to the serfs, who became land-owning peasants and as such liable for the taxes from which the nobles had been spared. Since the monarchy made itself responsible for everything, it too was always short of money and kept trying one financial expedient after another. Its purpose was not deliberately to weaken the nobility by taxing it, and Tocqueville says that the policy followed was not one king's but an institution's. But it was unreasonable to weaken the nobility in effect so far that its privileges appeared to be groundless, for when the Revolution came the nobility was unable to defend not only itself but the monarchy as well. The policy of the monarchy was not really a well-conceived strategy but ambition and avarice set loose and made regular in relentless centralization, which appeared to make government more rational but in reality made it less so. The monarchy did not realize that its anti-aristocratic policy would transform the nobility into a privileged caste rather than a working aristocracy—a distinction Tocqueville insists on. It did not see that its policy was effectually democratic and might actually lead to democracy.

While centering on the nobility, Tocqueville rounds out his description of the Old Regime with comments on the middle class, who imitated the nobility; on the peasants, who hated the nobility; and on the clergy, who did not take the side of the nobility. He allows that the French nobility, for all its decay, kept its pride and because of its "manly virtues" was neither servile nor given to the soft passion for material well-being that prevailed in his day. The nobles, with their ancient loyalty to the king, were able to call their souls free—a fact, he says, almost incomprehensible to the modern mind. They had a certain greatness, but they did not have political liberty. The kings they served were not cruel but mild; they did their best for the good of France and only stepped on those they did not notice. By their hostility to political liberty, they had denied themselves the means of learning what they were doing.

With this modulation of his argument, Tocqueville wants to leave the example of the nobles, even after his criticisms, as something positive for his day, capable of inspiring or shaming an electorate that had put Louis Napoleon in power. He attacks Burke, however, for supposing that the French nobility was still viable, if reformed, at the time of the Revolution. One could say in Burke's defense that he had Tocqueville's motive for praising the French nobility in a higher degree. Burke supposed that the British nobility was still viable in his time and did not want to impugn the viability of nobility as such; he had written his *Reflections on the Revolution in France* to kill sympathy for the French Revolution in Britain and to forestall the desire of British radicals to bring it across the Channel. Burke would certainly not have wanted to endorse Tocqueville's view that the new world of democracy was irresistible, nor did he. Yet for him too, in his famous phrase, the "age of chivalry is gone," the age when nobles would have leapt to the defense of Marie Antoinette. Perhaps his best option, in his version of Tocqueville's political history, was to exaggerate the soundness of nobility, just as Tocqueville's was to exaggerate its obsolescence and deny that it could have been reformed. A limited admiration without nostalgia could sum up Burke's view.

Tocqueville concludes his inquiry into the Old Regime with the judgment that it was not a whole, that it did not constitute a "nation." The feudal order in its heyday was a nation because it was a whole; it had unity through its parts. But the Old Regime became a unity of a different kind, without diverse parts but composed of individuals who were all the same. This was again perhaps not the intention of the monarchy, but it was the result. Its policy made France into a "frozen body" (*corps glacial*), a "uniform crowd" of "similars," each group separated and isolated from one another. He calls this condition "individualism," the concept he had used to such effect in his book on democracy. The Old Regime, he says, was a "sort of collective individualism, which prepared souls for the true individualism we are acquainted with."

True individualism is democratic, while the collective sort prepares it by educating individuals in the many small groups in the Old Regime to think only of themselves. Both collective and true individualism, one may suppose, are under the "government of one alone," whether a king or the abstract state of big government. "One alone" reminds of Montesquieu's *un seul* and Machiavelli's *uno solo*, referring to the despot or prince who establishes order. For Tocqueville, despotism is false, imposed order that does not cohere. To make a whole, a nation in the true sense, a people must have the political liberty to express and give form to its diverse parts. Political liberty is not the enemy of unity and order but, on the contrary, their necessary condition. It resists rule but also in the same voice claims to rule. The false unity imposed by one at the top, characteristic of democratic big government as much as of absolute monarchy, is open to revolution and deserves to be so. For Tocqueville, the French Revolution was both a sign of health and a culmination of disease—the health being in the attempt to make a whole and the disease in its predestined failure. It was surely more the establishment than the overthrow of authority, but the authority constructed by the Revolution was not legitimate because it did not succeed in making a whole.

The men of letters

Volume 3 of *The Old Regime*, its last part, is on the more particular and more recent facts that determined the place, birth, and character of "the great revolution," as Tocqueville now calls it. These could be considered the precipitating cause as opposed to the underlying cause, which was the administrative policy of the French monarchy. These facts turn out to be one fact, the men of letters who dominated French politics from the middle of the eighteenth century, together with their influence on the nobility, the clergy, and the king. Their central importance raises again the question of the role of ideas in politics for Tocqueville, the question that seemed central to *Democracy in America* but was left undecided there. Whether to act or to write is the question of Tocqueville's personal life, and the answer to that question is affected by the question whether writing is a form of acting, whether the ideas written down by an author can have political effect. He comes back to this matter in *The Old Regime*.

France had always been the most literary nation in Europe, but before the Revolution its men of letters developed a new obsession with politics. French men of letters were not involved with politics, as were their counterparts in England; they had no authority or public function. But they occupied themselves constantly with political things, always thinking abstractly, discussing such matters as the origin of societies, the primordial rights of citizens as opposed to authority, natural versus artificial relations among men, the legitimacy of custom, and the principles of laws. All of them thought it would be appropriate to substitute simple and elementary rules, taken from reason and natural law, for the complicated, traditional customs prevailing in the society of their time. Such abstract topics and this simplistic conclusion showed not only a lack of political experience but a contempt for it that was anathema to Tocqueville.

Tocqueville does not seek to explain this recent cause by looking to the history of modern political philosophy, where, as he well knew, he could have found that the search for simplicity in politics was initiated by Hobbes and Locke, with the cooperation of Descartes, who is cited in *Democracy in America*. Instead he asks why this idea, which he says was not new but three thousand years old, came to mind especially at this time. To answer, he cites the view the men of letters had of a society of unjust privileges, which "naturally led" them to want to rebuild society on an entirely new plan traced by each by the light of his own reason. They lacked the experience of free politics that might have warned them of the power of existing facts to hinder the most desirable forms, for the complete absence of all political liberty was invisible to them, and they could not know what they did not know. Tocqueville seems concerned to make the political authority responsible for the intellectual ascendancy of such foolishness, rather than to blame the men of letters for being the fools they were.

Who were the men of letters? Tocqueville mentions Voltaire of course, noting that he appreciated England for its free speech rather than for its political liberty. He does not mention Rousseau here, though Rousseau was as celebrated as Voltaire and much more cited by the revolutionaries themselves—as well as a favorite author of Tocqueville's. He gives the central role to the "economists," or physiocrats, who meddled irresponsibly with silly nostrums, showing zeal for equality and a tepid desire for liberty. The chief of them was Turgot, not a meddler but a man with "greatness of soul" and "rare qualities of genius" that distinguished him from all the others. Yet it was he who foolishly advised Louis XVI in 1775 that he could safely give the nation the shadow of freedom in an elected assembly without allowing it any powers. The economists promoted "democratic despotism" and inspired the socialism Tocqueville knew in his day. By making liberty a means to some other good such as equality or wealth, they helped induce the French people to lose their taste for it. "This sublime taste," he says in the chapter devoted to the economists, is the privilege of "great hearts" as opposed to the "mediocre souls" who have never felt it.

The economists had predecessors in the seventeenth century, above all Hobbes, but Tocqueville treats them as new. Their ideas may not be new, but they are newly relevant. He says that the men of letters became so influential that they shaped the French outlook on life, giving it a "singular education." The French nation was so alienated from its own affairs, so deprived of experience, that it easily succumbed to their influence. Even the nobles made way for writers, who became the primary political power, taking the place normally held by party chiefs in free countries. When the revolutionaries appeared on the scene, they echoed the same abstract theories—on which Tocqueville comments that "what is quality in a writer is often a vice in a statesman."

This remark applies especially to the attacks on the church preached by the men of letters, the most prominent feature of the education they taught. The church represented tradition, authority, and hierarchy—everything that the men of letters opposed in politics. They saw the church not as a potential ally of liberty, as did Tocqueville, but rather as the main obstacle to political revolution and reform. The church, however, had lost much of its force in the eighteenth century. It did not suppress, it merely irritated the writers with censorship that was not effective and with petty persecutions that alarmed them rather than silencing them. Indeed in that time, he says, it was believers who were silenced. The men of letters wanted a free press for their own sake so as to propose their simplistic reforms rather than liberty for all, a political liberty that might hinder or bring opposition to their plans. Revolutionary only in thought, none of them believed in violence, or had any clue that it might be looming ahead, or considered that they might be responsible for it. Tocqueville, however, holds them responsible for the character of the Revolution that came—not so much as men of ideas but as feckless statesmen who stumbled upon a political void and pranced with delight when they should have trembled with alarm.

When it comes to the men of letters with their abstract theories, Tocqueville joins with Edmund Burke to denounce them. But his attitude toward philosophy differs significantly, though subtly, from Burke's. While Burke attacks philosophy as such in order to oppose those who called themselves *philosophes* and then to replace it with a renewed faith in prudence, Tocqueville keeps quiet about philosophy and philosophical ideas as such, occasionally deprecating them for their impracticality, while offering a supplement to the good sense of prudence. This is the "great science of government" that teaches how to understand the general movements of society, to judge the mind of the masses, and to foresee what might result. He says that the first American he could meet on the street would know that religion is essential to a free society, because those least versed in the "science of government" know this much. Yet he never explains these striking references to political science, just as in *Democracy in America* he never supplies the "new political science…needed for a world altogether new" that he seems to promise at the beginning. An elaborated political science would derogate—steal the scene— from the activity of politics and might also infringe on the reader's liberty to think for himself. It is "the play of free institutions" that really teaches statesmen their art. Tocqueville's political science modestly refrains from making itself visible, or at any rate prominent, as a teacher of politics.

In the third part of *The Old Regime* Tocqueville does give an example of his political science, though it is not identified as such. This is his famous thesis that "the most dangerous moment for a bad government is ordinarily when it begins to reform itself." A people will tolerate oppression without complaint when it seems there is no escape from it, but when they see the prospect of relief, they become impatient and turn violent. Only in 1780, when reform was in the air, was the "theory of man's continual and indefinite perfectibility" born. That theory renders a people insensible of existing goods and impels it toward "new things." Here is the same irrational theory of progress studied in *Democracy in America*, now shown as a cause of revolution in France. Tocqueville praises the revolutionaries for their "admirable" belief in the perfectibility and power of man; they had passion for the glory of humanity and faith in its virtue. But if their hearts were sincere, their minds were disoriented by the abolition of divine laws and the overturning of civil laws. Progress toward perfectibility can be inspiring, but it never ends. Humans need a politics that sees a whole and man having a place within it if they wish to find satisfaction in liberty.

Chapter 6
Tocqueville's pride

In view of Tocqueville's criticisms of philosophy, it may seem
paradoxical and presumptuous to call him a philosopher. But he calls
himself a "new kind of liberal," and he sets forth a new liberalism that
he has rethought. In *Democracy in America* he criticizes materialist
philosophy for encouraging democracy's habit of finding nothing
in life but material pleasure and for depriving it of the pride excited
by religion. In *The Old Regime* he criticizes rationalist philosophy
for seeking systems of reform without caring about liberty. It is not
hard to see the two philosophies as aspects of the modern political
philosophy that is the source of liberalism: materialism for the sake
of reform rather than resignation to the inevitable, and rationalism
for the material improvement of life rather than contemplation.
Now in the *Recollections* [*Souvenirs*] Tocqueville displays the pride
he wants to add to liberalism, his own somewhat rueful pride, in an
account of the Revolution of 1848 in France, which he witnessed and
acted in. It is an account of failure, so hardly a triumph of pride. But
it is also instructive to philosophers who fancy themselves statesmen
and to citizens who let themselves be inspired by philosophers.

For myself alone?

Tocqueville's *Recollections* differs markedly from his two other
major works and was composed in between them, in 1850–51.
At the beginning he says he has been "removed momentarily

from the theater of affairs" and is unable to pursue any continued study because of his health. In October 1849 he had been forced to resign his office as Minister of Foreign Affairs, the highest and last post he was to hold in politics, which he held only for five months; then, in March 1850, he spat up blood for the first time, the sign of the disease that was to claim his life nine years later. He is alone now, "in the midst of my solitude," he says dramatically in the manner of Rousseau, and he decides to retrace the events of 1848 and to "paint the men" he saw taking part in them. This is not at all to be "a work of literature," like his other books, written for an audience; it is "for myself alone" (*pour moi seul*). And the *Recollections* was indeed shown but to a few friends, and published not during his lifetime but only in 1893 by the permission granted in his will.

This writing, Tocqueville says, will be a "mirror" in which he looks at his contemporaries and himself, not a "painting" destined for the public. His only goal is to procure "a solitary pleasure" for himself, to "contemplate alone" a true portrait of society and to see "man in the reality of his virtues and vices, to understand his nature and to judge it." So that his words may be sincere, he must keep them "entirely secret." Here is an emphatic distinction between looking in a mirror by himself—what he will do—and making a painting for others, which he will not do. And yet he has already said that he will "paint" the men he has seen, and in the next paragraph he speaks again of the events he wants to "paint." Moreover, in the rest of the book he goes on to "paint" men and events in his most brilliant style, not at all for his own amusement only. Though in a letter he describes the work as "daydreaming" (*revasserie*), he in fact consulted other actors and checked documents to verify his memory as well. Why the equivocation in his intended audience for this work?

The *Recollections* is indeed a painting, but for the next generation. Its many striking portraits of individuals are the distinctive feature of this work—by contrast to the other two books, which study causes and mention individuals only to illustrate generalizations. Here, starting with his mordant analysis of King Louis-Philippe, the reader is treated to one memorable, epigrammatic sketch after another of individuals not in command of events but victimized by their faults and sometimes by their virtues. Neither family (his sister-in-law) nor friend (J.-J. Ampère) is spared, and near the end of the book comes a devastating portrait of President (soon to be Emperor) Louis Napoleon as half an old conspirator, half an epicurean lover of easy pleasures. To publish these delights during his lifetime would have been the soul of indiscretion and would probably have cost him his liberty, but to record them for the next generations enables Tocqueville to show how practical politics actually works. In *Democracy in America* and *The Old Regime*, he extols the practice of political liberty; here he shows it at work—or rather, shows it failing to be established in France.

More than that, Tocqueville shows himself at work, or rather in failure. He himself is a man of letters in politics, like those he denounces in *The Old Regime*. Now he shows how far the man of letters can go in guiding politics, how much he depends on chance, how greatly he depends on the cooperation of mediocrities with whom he must work. This is the mirror aspect of the *Recollections* working in harmony with, but also in contrast to, the painting aspect, for when he looks at himself he sees a painter who is both in politics and above it as an instructor. At the end of *Democracy in America*, he says he had striven to enter into the point of view of God in order to judge between democracy and aristocracy. But he also said that God, unlike men, sees singular events as well as generalities. Here he looks at humanity from the side of individuality, for events are singular because individual human beings are diverse. The philosopher in politics, like the men of letters in eighteenth-century France, is inclined to think that general truths can be systematically applied to produce permanent improvement in human affairs. Thus a general truth can command obedience from particular circumstances and force them to do its will.

9. A sketch by Tocqueville of himself and his colleague Lanjuinais yoked to the ministry.

Tocqueville shows in his *Recollections* that this obedience will not occur. He puts himself in a situation, the 1848 Revolution in France, where he, a man of letters or a philosopher, wanted to control events but was unable to do so. Of course he opposed the theoreticians, above all the socialists, who wanted that revolution, and he did not claim to represent "philosophy" or indeed anything but himself. But in opposing the Revolution he took upon himself the role of counter-philosopher, who brings out the perversity of presuming philosophers. The 1848 Revolution overthrew the monarchy of Louis-Philippe, a result that Tocqueville vainly opposed, and then established a republic weakened by partisanship, in whose government he joined responsibly but not eagerly. The republic was in turn overthrown by Louis Napoleon in 1851, who reestablished Napoleon's empire, now become a mild, democratic despotism combining administrative centralization and bourgeois complacency. The 1848 revolutionaries did not get what they wanted, but neither did Tocqueville. He saw the worst of his predicted fears realized and was close enough to the crucial events to offer his own example of the impotence of a thinker. By not publishing his *Recollections* of these events until much later, he allows us to see inside his mind and to judge as he did, seeing these events unconcealed by the soothing platitudes required to please an audience of contemporaries.

Tocqueville gives a critical example of the failure of his advice. Though hardly an enthusiast for the monarchy, he believed it was better for France to maintain a constitutional monarchy with an elected assembly than to risk having a republic with an elected president that would open the way for a successor to Napoleon— the very thing that happened. The monarchy was overthrown by a violent invasion of the constitutional assembly (the Chamber of Deputies) by an armed mob on February 24, 1848. This event legitimated the right of a mob in Paris to act in the name of the French people and to use revolutionary violence against the constitution, and in reaction, it later drove the middle class and peasants into supporting Louis Napoleon to protect their property against that threat.

10. A mob storms a barricade during the 1848 Revolution in France. Tocqueville both foretold and opposed the Revolution but did not succeed in preventing it.

Tocqueville, a member of the Chamber of Deputies, was there on that day and tells of it in the *Recollections*: as the mob gathered he looked around for someone who could attempt to pacify the mob and fixed on Alphonse de Lamartine, poet, historian, and at that moment the most popular politician in the assembly. Tocqueville went to him and whispered in his ear that "we shall be lost" if you do not stand up to speak now. Lamartine refused; he would do nothing that might save the monarchy or risk his popularity. He spoke later, but too late, and the chance for safety was lost. A small troop of National Guards arrived, Tocqueville says, also a half-hour too late. Tocqueville was where he needed to be, but his advice was not taken and the result "changed the destinies of France." This is a drama somewhat contrived, perhaps, but with a purpose. It shows the limitations on the political scientist's advice, on possible reform, and on the blessings of political liberty. In the other two published books, Tocqueville praises the accomplishments of politics in America and condemns the lack of them in France, but the work unpublished in his lifetime ends with the sardonic statement that after two hard-earned successes in foreign affairs, the cabinet he belonged to fell. In that work he lets the constraints on politics, on the durability of political liberty, be known—but a long time later.

Socialism

Democracy does not fare well in the *Recollections*. Tocqueville says that in writing this work he wants to "keep the liberty to portray [paint] without flattery," and since he does not praise the justice of democracy in it as he does in *Democracy in America*, one might have to infer that he was flattering democracy in that book. When he exposed the petty bombast of political discussion in America, he contrasted it with the power of a "great orator discussing great affairs in a democratic assembly," but in this work he confesses:

> I have always thought that mediocre men, as well as men of merit,
> have a nose, a mouth, and eyes, but I have never been able to fix

in my memory the particular form of these features in each one of
them. I am constantly asking the names of these unknowns whom
I see every day, and I constantly forget them...I honor them, for
they lead the world, but they bore me profoundly.

This is not the attitude of a statesman eager or able to please.
Beyond this unintended disdain lies Tocqueville's judgment that
"socialism will remain the essential character and most fearsome
remembrance [*souvenir*]" of the 1848 Revolution. For a long time
the people had been gaining power, and it was inevitable that,
sooner or later, they would confront the privilege of property as
the main obstacle to equality. Socialism would seem to be the
next stage of the democratic revolution that he made the theme
of *Democracy in America*. His appraisal of the 1848 Revolution
as socialist contrasts markedly with Karl Marx's verdict in his
pamphlet *The Eighteenth Brumaire of Louis Napoleon* (1852),
who condemned it as a petty bourgeois farce. Marx was obliged to
fit his disappointment into his theory of history, which he did by
remarking that when history repeats itself (as his authority Hegel
had said), it is as farce after a tragedy. The tragedy was the French
Revolution of 1789, and by "tragedy" Marx meant not the Terror of
1793 but the Thermidor reaction against it. Tocqueville follows his
appraisal with an opposite reflection on the general disgust with
socialism in 1848, saying that it may return because the future
is more open than men who live in each society imagine. He of
course regarded property, especially petty bourgeois property,
as necessary to political liberty, while Marx was hostile to it just
because it sustained the delusion of political liberty.

Socialism to Tocqueville is a combination of passion in the people
and illusions in men of letters, with their "ingenious and false
systems," a later generation of those he will denounce in *The Old
Regime*. The literary spirit in politics consists in seeing what
is ingenious and new more than what is true, in preferring an
interesting tableau to a useful one, in showing oneself sensitive to
actors who play and speak well regardless of the consequences of

the play, and in deciding on the basis of impressions rather than reasons: all things he saw in his friend, the literary scholar Ampère, and perhaps would have seen in the surlier character of Marx.

The illusions of system, ridiculous in themselves, are not harmless in practice, yet Tocqueville has greater admiration for those who might revolt than for careless theorists of revolution. With more of the "painting" of individuals featured in the *Recollections*, he presents a tableau from his household contrasting his porter (not named) and his valet, Eugene. The porter was an old soldier of bad reputation in the neighborhood, a little loony, a good-for-nothing who spent all his time in a bar when he was not beating his wife—in sum, a socialist by birth or temperament. During the insurrection of June 1848, this man went around one day with a knife threatening to kill Tocqueville when he next saw him. But when Tocqueville returned in the evening, the porter did nothing and showed he had meant all along to do nothing. During revolutions, Tocqueville remarks, people boast of imaginary crimes just as in ordinary times they boast of imaginary good deeds. Eugene, however, was a soldier in the National Guard on the other side, who with great calm continued to perform his duties as valet while serving in the army of repression. He was not a philosopher but had the equanimity of one. Nor was he a socialist, but if socialism had won out, he, with his lack of restiveness and facile adjustment, would have become one. Achieving socialism calls forth qualities of spiritedness that will disappear under socialism.

The 1848 Revolution was not intended by the theorists whose theories called for a reform that could only be accomplished by revolution. Nor was it foreseen except by Tocqueville in a manifesto in October 1847 and in a warning speech in the Chamber of Deputies on January 27, 1848, a month before the event. "Do you not sense—what should I say—a breeze of revolution in the air?" he exclaimed. Taking up in the *Recollections* a theme of his other two books, he distinguishes general causes from particular accidents and finds six of each in the making of the Revolution. Men of letters fasten on general causes, particularly those "absolute systems," which he says he hates, "narrow in their pretended grandeur and false in their air of mathematical truth." Political men, by contrast, living in the midst of daily events, attribute everything to incidents in which they are involved. Tocqueville states that many historical facts have occurred by chance, or by such a mixture of secondary causes as amounts to chance, but that chance does nothing that has not been prepared in advance. The preparation in general causes can be foreseen, perhaps, only by a genius like Tocqueville, not with uncanny foresight but because his extraordinary vision is not obscured by the delusion of a system that diminishes all causes and every chance to a theory that is his, as if he were in charge of the universe. The literary spirit in politics is that of a tyrant, and the best check against it is the stubbornness of fact, sustained by the unpredictability of chance.

Chance and greatness

To the extent that chance determines, so far can human virtue intervene, for chance is what could have been otherwise and virtue requires scope for action. When virtuous people act, they replace what would have happened by chance, or by the mediocre actions of those not virtuous. So virtue has the intent of "banishing" chance, as Tocqueville says in *Democracy in America*. But virtue also presupposes chance so as to be able to replace it. In the deterministic, scientific systems Tocqueville rejects there is room for neither chance nor virtue. Virtue is not virtue if it is compelled; it must be voluntary, the virtuous person must be free. Virtue is the best indicator of liberty because a bad use of liberty, for example the corruption in French government under the monarchy of Louis-Philippe, is likely to be compelled, not free—as in this case by the passion for material enjoyments that so characterized that regime.

Yet Tocqueville is not a virtue salesman, touting his product as the only true liberty. His new kind of liberalism does not take the way of Kant toward a universal, categorical moral law that will express and guarantee liberty. Looking at actual individuals in the *Recollections*, he is impressed with the limits of human virtue. It is in the first place rare, and it is divided into public and private virtues so that an individual may have one set without the other, even that one set gets in the way of the other. Honesty is the virtue most in supply, but when action is required, a "bold rascal" may be worth more than an honest man. Democrats hardly ever fail to mix "nonsense" with their honesty. Madame de Lamartine Tocqueville found to be a woman of "true virtue," but to her virtue "she added almost all the defects that can be incorporated in it and that without changing it make it less agreeable." In *Democracy in America* he said that the "idea of rights is nothing other than the idea of virtue" in politics, but he does not discuss rights in the *Recollections*.

Instead, Tocqueville dwells on the distinction between petty and great; the bourgeois monarchy that was overthrown, the republic of socialism that was threatened but never accomplished, and the second Napoleonic empire were all triumphs of the petty over the great. Throughout Tocqueville's writings greatness is the inspiration of liberty, and greatness can be said to be the main feature of his "new kind" of liberalism. The desire for greatness is the motive that justifies and ennobles democratic patriotism, even democratic imperialism and colonialism.

Much attention has been given recently to Tocqueville's writings on Algeria endorsing French colonialism, a position thought to injure his reputation as a friend of democracy. But he approves of French colonialism in Algeria (of course without the use of slavery) as the expression of a desire for greatness necessary to dignify democracy above the assertion of a mediocre universal equality. He agrees with his friend John Stuart Mill that "civilization" is above "barbarism," though they might have quarreled over whether the superiority goes so far as to justify despotism, as Mill said in his book *On Liberty*. Still, the distinctness of democratic nations and the consequent glory of democratic patriotism point to the possibility of colonialism, should any of them develop a "civilizing mission" (not a phrase of Tocqueville's). The solution today is to drop the distinction between civilization and barbarism, thus transforming civilization into "culture." Cultures are all equal, and so the idea of multiculturalism today has nothing to say about greatness. Multiculturalism then becomes comparable to globalization, both of them apolitical in their intent to override political divisions, and thus hostile to Tocqueville's insistence on political liberty, requiring distinct political bodies. Insofar as political liberty is inspired by the desire for greatness, it risks embarking on enterprises to do good for others when the beneficiaries might have preferred to do good for themselves.

If Tocqueville is a new kind of liberal because he always has his eye on human greatness, why does he remain any kind of liberal? Is not greatness inescapably aristocratic, so that with greatness always in view he is not really a liberal at all—to say nothing of a democrat? To answer, one may compare him with Aristotle, who cannot be accused of being a liberal. Tocqueville agrees with Aristotle that man is by nature a political animal. He never repeats Aristotle's definition, but he clearly abandons the liberal alternative to it, first found in Hobbes, that man is by nature free and comes under politics only by consent to an artificial sovereign. Where then does he depart from Aristotle?

The departure can be seen precisely in the idea of human greatness that Tocqueville advances as distinct from virtue and human goodness in Aristotle. For Aristotle the good is sovereign because everything we humans aim at we *think* is good, and Aristotle extends this human view to all nature. But the sovereignty of the good is what Hobbes, the first liberal, denies. He posits that all of us desire self-preservation, the good we have in common, but we use our self-preservation in diverse ways to pursue goods we diversely opine to be good. There is no single highest good, but only a distinction between the minimum universal good, self-preservation, and the various goods we pursue according to our opinions. In politics, this makes for the fundamental, liberal distinction between the state, which secures the minimum good, and society, where we differ and live in what is today called pluralism.

Tocqueville takes this liberal route, following Hobbes and departing from Aristotle and classical political thought generally. But, agreeing with Aristotle, he holds on to the soul, and he speaks of "degraded souls." Liberalism frowns on the soul because it joins the minimal good of preservation to the maximum goal of the good life. A degraded soul would be one at a considerable distance from the good life, quite distinct from the liberal view that a self has merely made its own choice to live as it pleases, that its worth cannot be measured by a single, allegedly true notion of the good life. But instead of the "good life" Tocqueville speaks of "greatness." What difference does this make?

Greatness is not in nature but is attributed especially to humans *by* humans; it refers to greatness in the view of humans, or as Tocqueville says, "human greatness." It is in part variable and arbitrary, but the aspiration to greatness and admiration of it are in human nature. Only humans make judgments of what or who is important, and greatness is what humans consider important. It is distinguished from many merely useful things that are good and therefore are part of "goodness" but may be unimportant. Greatness is possible without virtue, as he says of Napoleon that he "was as great as one can be without virtue." With virtue one might be greater, but virtue is rare. Greatness is rare too, but being what humans consider important, which they do in various, often conflicting ways, it is more diverse than virtue, hence more compatible with political liberty. All have some notion of what is great, as what they look up to. But there is no necessary unity or consistency to "great" as there is to "good." That is why it would be rejected as sovereign by the classical thinkers. Greatness is also an accomplishment of practice, not theory. When Aristotle described the great-souled man, he was speaking of the realm of moral virtue in practice, as opposed to the intellectual virtue of a philosopher. Philosophers may have their notion of the greatness of the whole of nature, but they would use it to disparage the things most men consider great. Tocqueville remains with most men on this point. His distrust of philosophy is revealed in his insistence on greatness. Perhaps he has a hidden philosophy somehow akin to Aristotle's to justify his neglect of philosophy, a philosophy in defense of politics. But for the most part he finds it necessary to defend politics through disparagement of philosophy, for the liberal philosophy he knew was now the greatest danger to liberty and liberalism.

References

Preface

For the phrase "new kind of liberal," see AT's letter to Eugène Stoeffels, July 24, 1836, and for analysis of it, see Roger Boesche, *The Strange Liberalism of Alexis de Tocqueville* (Ithaca, NY: Cornell University Press, 1987). On AT's influence, see Raymond Aron, *Main Currents in Sociological Thought*, vol. 1 (New Brunswick, NJ: Transaction Publishers, 1998, orig. 1967), François Furet, *In the Workshop of History*, chap. 10 (Chicago: University of Chicago Press, 1984). Translations of AT's *Democracy in America* (hereafter *DA*): Harvey C. Mansfield and Delba Winthrop, trans. and eds. (Chicago: University of Chicago Press, 2000), and Arthur Goldhammer, trans. (New York: Library of America, 2004). Many of his letters can be found translated in Roger Boesche, ed., *Alexis de Tocqueville: Selected Letters on Politics and Society* (Berkeley: University of California Press, 1985). A sampling of current scholarship on AT is in *The Cambridge Companion to Tocqueville*, Cheryl B. Welch, ed. (New York: Cambridge University Press, 2006).

Chapter 1

The soundest biography of AT is André Jardin, *Tocqueville, A Biography* (New York: Farrar, Straus and Giroux, 1988); more recent is Hugh Brogan, *Alexis de Tocqueville, A Life* (New Haven, CT: Yale University Press, 2007). On the "great lottery of paternity," see AT's letter to his brother Edouard, September 2, 1840, and the somewhat different view in his letter to Louis de Kergorlay, November 11, 1833.

On his own ambition, see AT's letter to Mme. Swetchine, February 26, 1857. On AT's trip to America, see his notes in *Journey to America*, ed. J. P. Mayer (London: Faber & Faber, 1959), and the classic study of George W. Pierson, *Tocqueville and Beaumont in America* (New York: Oxford University Press, 1938). On mixing history and philosophy, see AT's letter to Kergorlay, December 15, 1850.

Chapter 2

Quotations follow the text in *Democracy in America* from the introduction through pt. 1 of vol. 1, then into pt. 2. The quotation on trading small virtues for the vice of pride is at *DA* vol. 2, pt. 3, chap. 19, and the one on the "two distinct humanities" is at *DA* vol. 2, pt. 4, chap. 8. On the writing of *Democracy in America*, see James T. Schleifer, *The Making of Democracy in America*, 2nd ed. (Indianapolis, IN: Liberty Fund, 2000). Pierre Manent, *Tocqueville and the Nature of Democracy* (Lanham, MD: Rowman & Littlefield, 1996), is the best overall study of the book, and Sheldon S. Wolin, *Tocqueville between Two Worlds* (Princeton, NJ: Princeton University Press, 2001) is an indispensable critique of AT. Careful readers will want to verify in the original texts the generalizations offered in this chapter about the liberalism of Hobbes and Locke, and in particular to explore the function of mores as argued in two of AT's favorite predecessors, Montesquieu (in the *Spirit of the Laws*, bk. 3, chap. 19) and Rousseau (in the *Social Contract*, bk. 2, chap. 12).

Chapter 3

Quotations are from pt. 2 of vol. 1. On AT's liberalism, see Pierre Manent, *An Intellectual History of Liberalism*, chap. 10 (Princeton, NJ: Princeton University Press, 1996). On AT's discussion of restlessness and its connection to Pascal, see Peter A. Lawler, *The Restless Mind: Alexis de Tocqueville on the Origin and Perpetuation of Human Liberty* (Lanham, MD: Rowman & Littlefield, 1993).

Chapter 4

Quotations follow the four parts of vol. 2 of *DA*. The phrase "immense being" can be found at *DA* vol. 2, bk. 1, chap. 7 and vol. 2, bk. 4, chap. 3. The argument for "two Democracies" can be found in Seymour Drescher, "Tocqueville's Two *Democracies*," *Journal of the History of*

Ideas 25 (1964): 201–16, and Jean-Claude Lamberti, *Tocqueville and the Two Democracies* (Cambridge, MA: Harvard University Press, 1989); the argument against, in Schleifer, *The Making of Tocqueville's Democracy*, 2nd ed. On religion, see Sanford Kessler, *Tocqueville's Civil Religion* (Albany: State University of New York Press, 1994), and Joshua Mitchell, *The Fragility of Freedom; Tocqueville on Religion, Democracy and the American Future* (Chicago: University of Chicago Press, 1995). On women, see Delba Winthrop, "Tocqueville's American Woman and 'the True Conception of Democratic Progress,'" *Political Theory* 14, no. 2 (1986): 239–61, and Cheryl Welch, *De Tocqueville* (Oxford: Oxford University Press, 2001).

Chapter 5

Quotations follow *The Old Regime and the Revolution* (hereafter *OR*) through its three parts. For the sources and analysis of *OR*, see especially Robert T. Gannett Jr., *Tocqueville Unveiled* (Chicago: University of Chicago Press, 2003). For analysis, see François Furet, *Interpreting the French Revolution* (Cambridge: Cambridge University Press, 1981), also Ralph Lerner, *Revolutions Revisited* (Chapel Hill: University of North Carolina Press, 1994). On "political history," see Delba Winthrop, "Tocqueville's Political History," *Review of Politics* 43 (1981): 88–111. Burke's most powerful attack on the French Revolution is his first analysis of it, *Reflections on the Revolution in France* (1790).

Chapter 6

Quotations from the *Recollections* again proceed from beginning to end of AT's text. For analysis, see Lawler, *The Restless Mind*. On Algeria, see Jennifer Pitts, ed., *Alexis de Tocqueville: Writings on Empire and Slavery* (Baltimore, MD: Johns Hopkins University Press, 2001), and Michael Hereth, *Alexis de Tocqueville: Threats to Freedom in Democracy* (Durham, NC: Duke University Press, 1986).

Index

A

Administration: centralized, 23–24, 79, 84, 91, 93–94; decentralized, 16, 24; rational, 1, 5, 84–87; as substitute for politics, 93

Algeria, 16, 111

America: aristocratic features of, 32–34; associations in, 26, 28, 37, 40, 52, 81–81, 94; decentralized administration in, 16, 24; freedom in, 3–4, 28, 33, 71; idea of progress in, 63–64, 71; jury in, 23; majority tyranny in, 41–42, 45; material well-being in, 51–52; no democratic revolution in, 68, 80; the people reign like God in, 20, 38, 41; philosophy in, 3, 59–60; the press in, 39; principal abode of democracy, 1, 5, 18–19, 91; pride in, 34–37, 44–45; religion in, 30–31, 61–62, 70, 100; self-interest in, 26–28, 68–69; spirit of manufacturing in, 65; three races in, 41–45; Tocqueville's trip to, 14–16, 39; townships in, 21–22, 37; writers in, 46; women in, 74–77

Ampère, Jean-Jacques, 14, 104, 109

Aristocracy: in America, 32–34, 71, 80–82; and associations, 21, 94; belief underlying, 36; contrasted with democracy, 9, 19, 21, 32, 39, 48–49, 52, 61, 64, 66–69, 72–73; democracy more just than, 86; in England, 16, 24, 33, 35, 61; greatness in, 81; in human nature, 39, 56, 67; Intendants in France as new, 92; loss of French, 5, 9, 86, 95; meaning of the word, 33–34; monarchical hostility to, 85, 95; pride in, 36, 50

Aristotle, 3, 33, 83, 112–14

Aron, Raymond, 5

Associations: American penchant for, 52, 78; art of, 26, 37; combat individualism, 21, 68, 79, 81–82; conjugal, 25, 76; political, 25–26, 40; and self-interest, 25–36; state hostility to, in France, 79, 92; as substitute for aristocratic persons, 32–33, 81–82, 94; theory of, 26; and virtue, 33; and the will of the people, 37, 40

F

G

H

Index

S

T

U